Why Can't I Make Money?

Why Can't I Make Money?

by Marta Merajver-Kurlat

Jorge Pinto Books Inc.
New York

Published by Jorge Pinto Books Inc., website: www.pintobooks.com
Cover design © 2010 by Nigel Holmes, website: www.nigelholmes.com
Book design by Charles King, website: www.ckmm.com

ISBN 978-1-934978-29-0
1-934978-29-9

BIBLIOTREATMENT SERIES

This book is not intended as a replacement for professional medical, dietary, financial, or psychiatric assistance, if that is needed.

Contents

Acknowledgments

I am deeply grateful to Jorge Pinto, whose advice and suggestions proved invaluable to the writing of this book.

I would also like to thank the men and women who kindly answered my questions and allowed me to use their experiences as a basis for the stories that illustrate the theory, as well as Psychoanalyst Claudia Lucía Borensztejn M.D., who provided insightful comments during the creation process.

M.M.K.

Introduction

You're probably reading this book because you found the title engaging. Still, the question in the title, though appropriate, doesn't come first on your list. You should be asking yourself, "do I really want to make money?" The answer is far from obvious. We all need money to live; we all need to earn money. However, making money has different connotations.

We all know what money is; unfortunately, we also believe we know what it *means*. As a lexical item, money is a portmanteau word that stands for a large number of unresolved unconscious issues.

In order to discover why you cannot make money, you will first need to uncover the connotations it has for *you*. Your first experiences of concrete money and/or verbal references about it in your presence will differ widely from other people's. Each experience is unique. Even though we may find similarities in members of a culture, social group, or family, ultimately the conditions in which the object money and its symbolic associations become a part of the unconscious respond to a particular concatenation of circumstances.

Typically, people who have trouble making money choose one of four paths to explain their failure. They blame it on their "bad luck," on the "system," on their own inadequacy, or on other, well-identified people who, out of envy, systematically prevent them from meeting their goals "when they are just about to make it."

Exception made of gambling, there is no such thing as "luck," good or bad. Interestingly, even the lottery, roulette, poker, etc. are called "chance games." For chance is the word. According to Answers.com, and considering the generalities only, chance may refer to an unpredictable element that seems to have no assignable cause, a force assumed to trigger events that cannot be foreseen or controlled, the likelihood of something happening, an accidental event, and a risk or hazard. Consider the explanations, with special attention to the words "seems" and "assumed." Their inclusion implies that there is a cause at the root of chance, but that the individual cannot find it. By the same token, "likelihood" speaks of probability, and probability refers the mind to statistics. That an event is accidental simply reminds us that it was not planned—at least, not that we know of. And risk lurks round every corner of our lives, since each step we take involves risk of some kind.

The term "system" is vague enough to avoid thinking of a clearly defined set of conditions. We live inside an economic system that weighs on the social structure, but ours is not a caste society. It is true that you may lock yourself up into a self-created caste and throw away the key. This must indeed feel much more comfortable than struggling up the ladder . . . if you don't mind the concomitant disadvantages. Perhaps you find pleasure in cursing the system; perhaps you derive enjoyment from complaining about your situation. Let me repeat this for the umpteenth time in this series: I don't know you. But you do, even if you think otherwise.

Inadequacy points to some lack. In this case, the lack of ability to make money. However, if you feel this is your problem, you need to accept that a lack of this kind is not genetic, incurable, or permanent. It originated at some point in your life, and for some specific reason. Amassing a fortune calls for a special talent, and I am willing to agree that talent is not learned. But we are not talking about fortunes here. The problem you don't seem to be able to overcome is far less complicated. On the other hand, if you have chosen the Rockefellers of this world as your role models, you are adding an extra problem, for then you are perhaps a dreamer who lets go of the bird in hand because of the hundred in the bush of your imagination.

Finally, there are those "others" who will not let you succeed. How has it come to occur to you that your economic success might become a threat to them? This image of yourself sounds, at best, delusional. You are no Bugsy Siegel out to replace Joe Masseria in the organized crime of the early 1930s. Shouldn't we turn the tables and wonder whether you're exceedingly angry that there are competitors in this race and that only the fittest will get to the finishing line? Is this not a prefabricated excuse to justify having quit halfway through?

Whatever you think are the reasons that keep you tied to underachievement (your words, not mine), you need to know that you can change; that is, as long as financial success is what you really want. Don't give me that "how-dumb-can-you-be" look. Before anything else, you need to make sure that, to you, making money is a genuine desire rather than a social or parental mandate. Journeying through these pages will acquaint you with the unconscious issues at work in your psyche, with a number of sentiments and fears concealed under a cloak labeled "money," with your personal symbolic world in regard to money, and with the freedom and responsibility of making a for or against choice.

1

1.1

The Dark Side of Money

One startling fact about money is that most of us would kill for it—some figuratively and others factually—notwithstanding the fact that money has had very bad press since early times.

In Book VIII of *The Republic*, speaking about the divine versus the human origin of our race, Plato wrote,

> When discord arose, then the two races were drawn different ways: the iron and brass fell to acquiring money and land and houses and gold and silver; but the gold and silver races, not wanting money but having the true riches in their own nature, inclined towards virtue and the ancient order of things. There was a battle between them, and at last they agreed to distribute their land and houses among individual owners; and they enslaved their friends and maintainers, whom they had formerly protected in the condition of freemen, and made of them subjects and servants; and they themselves were engaged in war and in keeping a watch against them. And men of this

stamp will be covetous of money, like those who live in oligarchies; they will have, a fierce secret longing after gold and silver, which they will hoard in dark places, having magazines and treasuries of their own for the deposit and concealment of them; also castles which are just nests for their eggs, and in which they will spend large sums on their wives, or on any others whom they please.

That is most true, he said.

And they are miserly because they have no means of openly acquiring the money which they prize; they will spend that which is another man's on the gratification of their desires, stealing their pleasures and running away like children from the law, their father: they have been schooled not by gentle influences but by force, for they have neglected her who is the true Muse, the companion of reason and philosophy, and have honoured gymnastic more than music.

And then one, seeing another grow rich, seeks to rival him, and thus the great mass of the citizens become lovers of money.

And so they grow richer and richer, and the more they think of making a fortune the less they think of virtue; for when riches and virtue are placed together in the scales of the balance, the one always rises as the other falls.

And in proportion as riches and rich men are honoured in the State, virtue and the virtuous are dishonoured.

Clearly.

And what is honoured is cultivated, and that which has no honour is neglected.

That is obvious.

And so at last, instead of loving contention and glory, men become lovers of trade and money; they honour and look up to the rich man, and make a ruler of him, and dishonour the poor man.

Does the above quotation ring a bell? Perhaps you have not read this text before, but I guess you can easily recognize contemporary society in Plato's description. You could argue that his times were eons away from ours, and plead a case against riches for riches' sake.

You could reasonably contend that the present (induced) need for consumption, added to the greedy organization of the Modern State, demands tons of money. The ancients, you might say, were into accumulation rather than into circulation. Everybody knows that our purchases keep the markets in motion, keep unemployment at bay, feed fair distribution programs, and the like. Being no economist, I'd rather draw the line right here. You are welcome to use the blank page/s at the end of this chapter to jot down your views of the underside of money. Forget your own predicament while you do so, and try to be as objective as possible.

In a number of cases, money is still about accumulation. The eyes of my mind cannot stop focusing on Donald's Uncle Scrooge wallowing in his gold-coin pool. If this is too old-fashioned, substitute hateful Mr. Burns in *The Simpsons* for it. Why do these characters find it so pressing to turn everything into money? Certainly not because of money itself, but because of the power it gives the possessor. Who would say "no" to such characters, besides lovable, idealistic, and not very true-to-life Lisa Simpson? No one. The common man is much too afraid of the consequences of opposing the powerful. The common man has never heard of King Midas. Just in case you haven't either, let me tell you the story.

Midas was a legendary king of Bromium to whom great wealth was predicted when, as a baby lying in his cradle, a procession of ants carrying grains of wheat marched into the room and deposited the grains between the lips of the sleeping infant. Years later, grateful for Midas having protected his pedagogue Silenus, the god Dionysus asked how the king wished to be rewarded. Without thinking twice of what he was asking, Midas replied, "Grant that all I touch be turned into gold." The god honored his request to the letter, and poor richest-man-in-the-world Midas came near to die of starvation, for even the food and drink he touched turned instantly into solid gold. This pushed some sense into his head, and he begged Dionysus to release him of his wish, which he did, advising him to bathe in the waters of a certain river. Apart from a serious interpretation of the myth into which we will not go, the moral of the story is that sometimes we do not really consider the true meaning and consequences of what we wish for. Had Dionysus been less benevolent, Midas would have literally choked on his ambition. Here you have a good example of "chance" and "risk" combined.

Going back to the common man, I very much doubt that, should he be familiar with this myth, he would make a different choice from Midas'. Moreover, he would probably think that he could manage to stay alive without foregoing the gold. Yes, you're right. Midas was already a powerful king before making his wish. But he figured—correctly— that more gold would make him more powerful. What for? To command more respect and allegiance from fellow kings and more admiration and awe from other men. Power is a deadly bane. Those who have had a taste of it crave for more, no matter what it takes. It develops into a dangerous addiction supported on a network whose "basic paste" happens to be money.

1.2

In much earlier times, the Hebrew culture also had something to say about money. Oh yes, the Jew stereotype has long been that of an avaricious hoarder, always ready to make the most of business opportunities. Yet this is a stereotype built when the Hebrews lost their homeland and had to integrate into other communities. They did not choose to deal in money. The alien societies amidst which they lived curtailed their rights to perform a number of activities, but graciously allowed them the "privilege" of loaning and trade. The reasons wielded in Babylon differed from those in medieval Europe, but the long and the short of it is that the Jew people had to earn their living like everyone else and, if money was the permitted tool, this tool they used.

However, the Old Testament speaks at length of money.

I'd like to quote some of its warnings and reflections on the matter. We can save the brighter views for the next chapter.

In an awesome book entitled *Los judíos, el mundo y el dinero,* Jacques Attali* extracts four of what he understands as Bible lessons in economy. Revisiting the myth of the Second Fall (that is, the Fall of Man, following the First Fall, i.e., that of the rebellious angels), he offers an economic interpretation about eating the forbidden fruit. In his view, this is when man awakens to self-awareness and to the desire to possess goods. His conclusion: it is desire that produces scarcity and not the other way around. In other words, when everyone has about the same, which may well be precious little, social and economic equilibrium are preserved. But as soon as desire raises its head, it will prompt dispossession of the weakest in favor of accumulation by the strongest or shrewdest.

Once out of Eden, the right to and care of the land and sheep (read the latter as animals for consumption) befalls to Adam and Eve's two elder children. Thus the two categories essential for survival are created: the peasant and the shepherd. The passage in Genesis is obscure. It does not seem clear why Abel found favor in the eyes of God:

> Now Abel kept flocks, and Cain worked the soil. In the course of time Cain brought some of the fruits of the soil as an offering to the LORD. But Abel brought fat portions from some of the firstborn of his flock. The LORD looked with favor on Abel and his offering, but

---

* Translated from French into English as *The Jews, the World, and Money.*

on Cain and his offering he did not look with favor. So Cain was very angry, and his face was downcast.

Then the LORD said to Cain, "Why are you angry? Why is your face downcast? If you do what is right, will you not be accepted? But if you do not do what is right, sin is crouching at your door; it desires to have you, but you must master it."

Now Cain said to his brother Abel, "Let's go out to the field." And while they were in the field, Cain attacked his brother Abel and killed him.

One explanation for God's behavior proposes that Cain had offered only a few linen seeds while Abel had chosen his best, fattest lamb. Were we to accept this version, we would be witnessing the birth of greed, its punishment, and the miser's reaction to his brother's generosity.

An alternative interpretation maintains that Cain and Abel stand for an agricultural and a nomadic cattle-raising society respectively, and that the source of the conflict lay in the fact that the peasants forbade the shepherds access to their lands. As neither would yield—allegedly, Cain ordered Abel to fly across his land, denying him the right to step on it, to which Abel replied that Cain should strip naked because the clothes he was wearing were made of sheepskin (his property)—one had to die.

Not bearing the above possibilities in mind, Attali concludes that everyone wishes to posses the same as others desire. In a religious sense, these two brothers desired the love of God; what offended Cain to the point of murder was God's manifest preference for Abel. The right of primogeniture* must also have inflamed his rage, though this is another cup of tea. In an earthly sense, it would seem as if the division of roles didn't make either of them happy. Both wanted to possess the whole of the available goods, one died, and the other was set loose in the world, supposedly to be persecuted for his crime to the end of his days.

Among the many stories told of Cain's lot, perhaps the most interesting to us is the one that declares that he never changed his ways. He accumulated money and power, spread the art of financial cheating, was the first to fence the fields round the many cities that he founded, and forced his numerous descendants to live within their walls and work for his profit.

In a way, a part of the human race could proudly claim kinship to Cain.

The book of Exodus narrates how the Hebrews succeeded in freeing themselves from bondage in the land of Egypt. Most fictional works on this episode, including movies and TV serials, emphasize the importance of Moses' leadership and the horror of the plagues that fell on the haughty Pharaoh and his people. Yet something important slipped

---

* Where common law applied, primogeniture was the right of the eldest son to inherit the whole of the estate. In the biblical stories of the origin, it also implied the unquestionable right to leadership. Although most Western countries have changed their legislation in various ways, the social imaginary still values the elder/eldest son as the continuer of the family name and the keeper of the father's/lineage's achievements, particularly if money is part of the picture. One can imagine that other offspring of the same family find themselves at a psychological disadvantage in regard to moneymaking unless their parents have boosted their self-confidence to persuade them of their own abilities to meet this and other goals.

through. After the last and most terrible plague (the death of all Egyptian firstborns), God ordered that,

> Every woman is to ask her neighbor and any woman living in her house for articles of silver and gold and for clothing, which you will put on your sons and daughters. And so you will plunder the Egyptians.

Though one might be naive enough to believe that the terrified survivors willingly gave up their treasures out of fear of these extraordinary people whose single God had proved to be a thousand times more powerful than their pantheon, this notion needs rethinking. The Egyptians hated parting with their property. They felt it was exacted from them through tacit threats of worse catastrophes, and bitterly resented transferring their riches to the slaves who, in their opinion, should have been allowed to leave before devastation preyed on their country.

Attali's construct of later events shows that when money is forcefully obtained through terror it tends to go along the same path. He means that the Egyptian gold and silver, the only precious metals available to build the sacrilegious Golden Calf in the desert while Moses stayed away on Mount Sinai, were burned to cinders by Moses' wrath. Furthermore,

> Moses saw that the people were running wild and that Aaron had let them get out of control and so become a laughingstock to their enemies. So he stood at the

entrance to the camp and said, "Whoever is for the LORD, come to me." And all the Levites rallied to him.

Then he said to them, "This is what the LORD, the God of Israel, says: "Each man strap a sword to his side. Go back and forth through the camp from one end to the other, each killing his brother and friend and neighbor." The Levites did as Moses commanded, and *that day about three thousand of the people died.* Then Moses said, "You have been set apart to the LORD today, for you were against your own sons and brothers, and he has blessed you this day."

Thus not only riches but also lives were lost. That the Golden Calf stood in open defiance of God's commandments that "You shall not make for yourselves an idol [. . .]" and "You shall not bow to them or worship them [. . .]" is clear enough. What is not so clear is why God ordered his people to plunder the Egyptians in the first place. Here I would suspect that the writing of the Scriptures, made at a much later time, tried to justify a human act urged by the desire to possess. At any rate, one is called upon to ponder the consequences of acquiring wealth at whatever cost.

In the context of the times, when the purpose of personal wealth is accumulation per se money or its equivalent competes with God, for it replaces Him as an object of worship. The Old Testament abounds in examples that, unless ruled by morality, becoming rich amounts to blasphemy:

Give me neither poverty nor riches,
but give me only my daily bread.

Otherwise, I may have too much and disown you
and say, "Who is the LORD?"

All in all, brimming with cautionary advice, the successive rewrites of the Old Testament, together with the Talmud (the debates on the law), ended up by agreeing that there was no harm in wealth as long as God and brethren had been given their due. Conversely, the advent of Christianity retraced the steps of Judaism, and once more money was viewed as an instrument of the devil. You may wonder why so much insistence on ancient history, or myth or whatever you feel the Bible stands for. Simply because, although you may not be aware of it, the foundations of your society lie heavily on an interpretation (or misinterpretation) of the reformation wave going by the general name of Protestantism.

So let's see what the first Christians thought of riches.

1.3
St. Matthew seemed to be extremely concerned about man's relation to money. Among other things, he said,

Do not save riches for yourselves here on earth, where moths and rust destroy, and robbers break in and steal. Instead, save riches for yourselves in heaven, where moths and rust cannot destroy, and robbers cannot break in and steal. For your heart will always be where your riches are.

* * *

No one can serve two masters. Either he will hate the one and love the other, or he will be devoted to the one and despise the other. You cannot serve both God and Mammon.

St. Luke seemed to take the issue more personally:

Only the man who says goodbye to all his possessions can be my disciple.

* * *

[John answered,] "The man with two tunics should share with him who has none, and the one who has food should do the same."

* * *

Give to everyone who asks you, and do not ask for your property back from the man who robs you.

* * *

St. Luke also makes a very specific point about money:

Now my advice to you is to use "money," tainted as it is, to make yourselves friends, so that when it comes to an end, they may welcome you into the houses of eternity. The man who is faithful in the little things will be faithful in the big things. So that if you are not fit to be trusted to deal with the wicked wealth of this world, who will trust you with true riches?

Why do you think St. Luke remarks that money is "tainted" and reinforces the idea by speaking of "the wicked wealth of this world"? It would seem as if, in the light of their own experience regarding the connections between money and corruption, the authors of the Gospels were unable to reconcile some positive feature of money with spiritual goodness and the true riches of eternal life.

Moreover, and to end with this brief yet telling revision of the Bible, we find the following passage in the Book of Revelations:

> While you say, "I am rich, I have prospered, and there is nothing that I need," you have no eyes to see that you are wretched, pitiable, poverty-stricken, blind, and naked. My advice to you is to buy from me that gold which is refined in the furnace so that you may be rich, and white garments to wear so that you may hide the shame of your nakedness, and salve to put on your eyes to make you see. All those whom I love I correct and discipline. Therefore, shake off your complacency and repent.

No doubt Jesus could flog the souls of the rich with the same harshness as he flogged the merchants in the Temple.

The sad thing is that money, being a lifeless object, is neither good nor bad in itself. The same has been argued about arms, although the big difference between wealth and guns resides in the fact that the latter, whether for defensive or offensive purposes, were devised to do great damage. Money was not created for harmful purposes but, according to the beliefs quoted in this chapter, it seems as if man's wicked ways have made wealth synonymous with the deadliest weapons.

In *Paradise Lost,* English poet John Milton, also a civil servant under Oliver Cromwell, that is, a Protestant, although his true religious leanings have raised much controversy, depicted Mammon, one of the fallen angels, as the epitome of cupidity.

Mammon led them on—
Mammon, the least erected Spirit that fell
From Heaven; for even in Heaven his looks and thoughts
Were always downward bent, admiring more
The riches of heaven's pavement, trodden gold,
Than aught divine or holy else enjoyed
In vision beatific. By him first
Men also, and by his suggestion taught,
Ransacked the centre, and with impious hands
Rifled the bowels of their mother Earth
For treasures better hid. Soon had his crew
Opened into the hill a spacious wound,
And digged out ribs of gold. Let none admire
That riches grow in Hell; that soil may best
Deserve the precious bane. And here let those
Who boast in mortal things, and wondering tell
Of Babel, and the works of Memphian kings,

Learn how their greatest monuments of fame
And strength, and art, are easily outdone
By Spirits reprobate, and in an hour
What in an age they, with incessant toil
And hands innumerable, scarce perform.
Nigh on the plain, in many cells prepared,
That underneath had veins of liquid fire
Sluiced from the lake, a second multitude
With wondrous art founded the massy ore,
Severing each kind, and scummed the bullion-dross.

This evil spirit has a Biblical origin as well, and in medieval times commonly personified the thirst for riches. From all the above, one could surmise that moral condemnation of wealth has been shared by the great thinkers and religious leaders from different historical eras. I sincerely hope that you are not beginning to blame yourself for having dared to entertain such an accursed wish. The coin has two sides. The next section intends to show you that at least one of these texts—perhaps the most significant one in terms of its universality—made a most convincing case for the advantages of legitimate personal wealth.

1.4

In defense of money

An anthropological study of the story of Abraham and Isaac would conclude that it allegorizes the end of human sacrifices in the culture described by Genesis. To the indignant voices that claim that the people who later went by the name of Hebrews did not indulge in such sacrifices, let me oppose a prohibition expressed in different words throughout the books gathered in the Old Testament: "And thou shall not let any of thy children pass through the fire to Moloch." There would be absolutely no reason to prohibit something that no one did in the first place. So yes, like all other incipient cultures these people (my people, by the way, just in case you're accusing me of anti-Semitism) went through the same evolutionary stages as others. At some point, animals took the place of humans at the sacrificial stone.

God tested Abraham, and said to him, "Abraham!" And he said, "Here am I." He said, "Take your son, your only son Isaac, whom you love, and go to the land of Mori'ah, and offer him there as a burnt offering upon one of the mountains of which I shall tell you." So Abraham rose early in the morning, saddled his ass, and took two of his young men with him, and his son Isaac; and he cut the wood for the burnt offering, and arose and went to the place of which God had told him. On the third day Abraham lifted up his eyes and saw the place afar off. Then Abraham said to his young men, "Stay here with the ass; I and the lad will go yonder and worship, and come again to you." And Abraham took the wood of the burnt offering, and laid it on Isaac his son; and he took in his hand the fire and the knife. So they went both of them together. And Isaac said to his father Abraham, "My father!" And he said, "Here am I, my son." He said, "Behold, the fire and the wood; but where is the lamb for a burnt offering?"

Abraham said, "God will provide himself the lamb for a burnt offering, my son." So they went both of them together. When they came to the place of which God had told him, Abraham built an altar there, and laid the wood in order, and bound Isaac his son, and laid him on the altar, upon the wood. Then Abraham put forth his hand, and took the knife to slay his son. But the angel of the LORD called to him from heaven, and said, "Abraham, Abraham!" And he said, "Here am I." He said, "Do not lay your hand on the lad or do anything to him; for now I know that you fear God, seeing you have not withheld your son, your only son, from me." And Abraham lifted up his eyes and looked, and behold, behind him was a ram, caught in a thicket by his horns; and Abraham went and took the ram, and offered it up as a burnt offering instead of his son.

Attali gives the episode an altogether different twist. According to him, God's purpose in saving Isaac's life was not to reward Abraham's blind obedience but to shift violence away from the loss of lives and direct it toward material possessions. Hence Attali declares that wealth is the best cure/replacement for violence. In other words, as long as you can offer money value, your physical integrity will not suffer.

The Lex Talionis (Talion Law), originated in the Code of Hammurabi and often referred to in the Torah by way of the paraphrase "an eye for an eye and a tooth for a tooth," should not be taken literally. I haven't found biblical examples of parts of the body being torn off in retaliation for injuries caused to others. Perhaps it was so in the Babylonian Empire, but among the Hebrews this bloody form of retribution was most probably a metaphor indicating that fair economic compensation should be paid for damages/losses affecting the injured party.

The Old Testament suggests that money (or its equivalent, for we are still far from the invention of coins and bills) is the right way to acquire necessary or desired goods without resorting to morally damnable practices. From this point of view, possessing money protects you from the temptation of committing a number of hateful crimes. Still, the Torah also makes it very clear that money should be earned in lawful ways, and establishes a system of distribution that ensures that the destitute will not go hungry, roofless, or naked.

All this was regulated together with the cult. Unfortunately, when the priests grew into a corporation, with a charter being the only missing element, they became exceedingly rapacious "in the name of God." One imagines that this is what Jesus and his disciples reacted strongly against, for the goodness deriving from money had been twisted out of recognition in detriment to the people.

However, the spell of blessed poverty did not last long, and the new Church, in turn, copied and perfected the exaction practiced by the abhorred Temple priests. In addition, there came a time when the belief that Jesus had preached poverty was regarded as heretic, probably because of contradictory accounts of his words in the four Gospels. In fact, while St. Luke makes Jesus utter the phrase "Blessed are you poor," St. Matthew has him say, "Blessed are the poor in spirit." What Jesus' actual words were will forever remain a mystery, but the lack of agreement between these two evangelists opened the door for the acceptance of earthly riches while justifying the pomp and splendor of the Catholic Church.

I.5

In the 16th century, German monk Martin Luther felt that the business conducted by the Church, particularly the sale of indulgences, had gone too far. He undertook the Reformation, to which there were many other contributors even before he collected his thoughts in a written corpus. The combination of the various reformers took the all-inclusive name of Protestantism.

In his study of Luther, Max Weber states that "that the fulfillment of worldly duties is under all circumstances the only way to live acceptably to God. It and it alone is the will of God, and hence every legitimate calling has exactly the same worth in the sight of God." It can easily be inferred that such fulfillment involves work and, therefore, wages or some other payment in money. John Wesley, the founder of Methodism, established some sort of equilibrium by advising that "we ought not to prevent people from being diligent and frugal; we must exhort all Christians to gain all they can, and to save all they can; that is, in effect, to grow rich."*

On contrasting Luther and Calvin, Weber shows us the predicament of those who adhered to Protestantism.

---

* Weber, Max. *The Protestant Ethic and the Spirit of Capitalism.*

Returning to the concept of predestination, though not in the Greek sense, Calvin maintained that man is predestined (or not) for salvation; in other words, chosen by God.

The question "Am I one of the elect?" must sooner or later have arisen for every believer and forced all other interests into the background. "And how can I be sure of my state of grace?" For Calvin himself this was not a problem. He felt himself to be a chosen agent of the Lord, and was certain of his own salvation. Accordingly, to the question of how the individual can be certain of his own election, he has at bottom only the answer that we should be content with the knowledge that God has chosen and depend further only on that implicit trust in Christ which is the result of true faith. He rejects in principle the assumption that one can learn from the conduct of others whether they are chosen or damned. "It is an unjustifiable attempt to force God's secrets. The elect differ externally in this life in no way from the damned; and even all the subjective experiences of the chosen are, as *ludibria spiritus sancti*, possible for the damned with the single exception of that *finaliter expectant*, trusting faith. The elect thus are and remain God's invisible Church."*

That "the elect differ externally in this life in no way from the damned" cannot have been easy to swallow. One solution to appease the anguish of not knowing in which group

---

* Jean Cauvin (John Calvin) cited by Max Weber in *The Protestant Ethic and the Spirit of Capitalism*.

believers in the reformed church belonged seems to have consisted in seeking material success to show that God was on their side (or that they would sit by God's side; at some point things turned really confusing.) They reasoned that, were they not among the elected, God would send some signal to deflect their course.

America cannot deny its Protestant roots. Even men like Benjamin Franklin devoted much of their time to making money without neglecting the accompanying qualities of thrift and frugality that were expected from a sincere commitment to God's plan. He even wrote a book entitled *The Way to Wealth*, containing a collection of sensible tips that have not become at all dated. "God helps them that help themselves" and "Get what you can, and what you get hold; 'tis the stone that will turn all your lead into gold" provide two interesting examples of his views on money.

Perhaps many Americans no longer remember that their connection to money stems from a religious quandary. The virtue alone seems to have remained. There may also be an unconscious split between their spiritual beliefs and their practical philosophy. Yet the fact remains that, regardless of this society's collective memory or lack thereof, ordinary people tend to divide the world into "winners" and "losers." The former are those who at least express a desire for wealth and act accordingly. The latter freeze in their desire or else fail in their attempts to make it come true. No one seems to consider the existence of individuals out of this classification. And this is the first thing *you* need to internalize: there are never only two ways to look at a situation.

I do not intend to persuade you that you should join the "winners." That is for you to decide once you have read about the possible reasons that are hindering you. Yet perhaps it would help to acquaint you with a little personal history, for you must be wondering what makes me the right person to talk about money. In other words, am I a "winner" or a "loser"?

To begin with, although it may sound as if I'm speaking about money, I am definitely not doing that. I have merely displayed a backdrop against which to play the drama of your anxiety. In addition, my society does not judge success exclusively from money but mostly from personal achievement, which often does not imply wealth. Then, I count among the winners because of my professional and career achievements, although my worldly possessions reflect a different reality. However, I will tell you this much: I firmly believe that those who really want to make money find a way to achieve their goal. So our task here is to provide you with tools that will enable you to answer the two important questions that matter to you. First, what do *you* want? And, second, if you truthfully want money, what in your unconscious mind is stopping you?

1.6

We can find a number of arguments in favor of money by just going over the dictates of daily life. Suppose you believe that "money is the root of all evils" and therefore decide you want nothing with it. Unless you are living in one of those communities that have gone back to producing everything they need to survive and meet their needs through barter, you must be taking advantage of someone else's money. How so? You're definitely not a bum. Perhaps you're an artist, a thinker, an inventor, someone who refuses to waste her invaluable time doing menial jobs while postponing her true, all-important calling. You feel you have the right to a patron, just as great men of former times did. Still, consider that even if you don't receive actual money from relatives or friends, the food you eat at their tables has cost money . . . *their* money. The same holds good if you're a non-paying guest at their homes. You consume gas, electricity, and water, to mention just a few kernel needs. Are you morally entitled to make other people spend money just because you feel you're intellectually above them?

If this is how you feel, you may be treading a similar path to Raskolnikov's, the wretched protagonist of Dostoevski's *Crime and Punishment.* In keeping with Nietszche's theory of the Superman*, Raskolnikov firmly believed in the existence of extraordinary men and ordinary men. In his sick mind, the former were not subject to any laws or rules while the latter served as fodder for the "extraordinary man" to fulfill his destiny of grandeur for the greater good. Following this line of thought, Raskolnikov, a young man forced to give up his university studies for lack of means (but he wouldn't demean himself to give lessons, for instance) planned and executed the murder of a money lender whom he regarded as a leech, a loathsome character whose life was, in his eyes, absolutely worthless. The murder was "necessary" to steal the woman's money and thus support himself, devoting all

---

* Developed in Nietzsche's *Thus Spake Zarathustra.*

his time to what mattered: the development of his superior intellect.

Although the novel makes relatively quick work of the crime and dwells at great length on Raskolnikov's suffering and his calvary toward atonement, it never stops reminding the reader that not for a moment did the ex student regret having killed the "scoudrel." I am not suggesting that you may go to such lengths. However, overt or not, exploitation of others under the pretext of belonging to the group of extraordinary men does, in fact, show a dangerously dishonest turn of character.

You read in section 1.1 that money amounts to control exerted over others. Yet there is a positive side to it when, through money, you can control your own life. In this sense, money gives you independence, freedom of decision, and the possibility of effectively disagreeing with others that might want to impose their standards on you because they hold the strings to the purse.

It is customary in your society for teenagers of all social classes to take on part time and/or summer jobs even if they don't really need the pittance they earn. This salutary custom teaches youngsters that money does not grow on trees, and that it takes time and (more often than not) hard work to earn the bills that parents in other societies gladly hand out until their offspring are "prepared to make a living." Your culture, because of the strong Protestant influence discussed before, regards the ability of earning money through work as a most commendable virtue to be encouraged at the earliest age possible. Therefore, in principle, if you have been raised in this way, there should be no reason for your rejecting the effort money implies. We'll come back to this "should be" later on in the text.

Especially in the case of women, there appears a rupture between their childless years and the moment they become mothers. Many women who found spiritual and material satisfaction at their jobs or careers have to interrupt their progress toward better positions in order to take care of their babies. Expert, reliable caregiving proves too expensive for most of these women, and even those who could afford it tend to prefer staying at home for a couple of years and watching over their young themselves. It would seem as if only those whose salary is essential to the family's survival leave their children in daycare. Perhaps the established conventions about the qualities of a "good mom" play a part in these decisions, or perhaps mothers actually feel more at ease when they undertake the task of raising their children until they have, for example, acquired enough of the language to talk about their experiences while in the care of strangers.

Whatever the reasons, a large number of these women find it exceedingly difficult to reenter the job market at the point where they left it once the children have started their school routine. And some simply cannot go back at all. A few years out of the game have set them back what looks like a century regarding technological advances, office procedures, and business strategies. In the meantime, they depend on their husbands' income or on their savings— supposing they have some—for large and small expenditures they deem necessary. What comes next? A way of living that, in their minds, appeared as temporary, becomes permanent. Everything they want or need for themselves and their children depends on their husbands' willingness to comply. As sometimes husband and wife don't see eye to eye on a number of issues involving money, some of these women either feel they are getting the worst part of the deal or resort to guile to obtain what they want/need. In both cases women feel humiliated and/or grow embittered, which is bad enough. A third possibility is that they may turn cynical and accept the new rules as unfair but inescapable. It goes without saying that such imbalance erodes the marriage. It doesn't matter whether or not the couple reaches the point of divorce. Many unpleasant situations stem from a woman's utter dependence on her husband's money, notably the refusal to have sex with him when her requests for money have met a negative answer or, conversely, the incitement to have sex in the hope of being "rewarded" with the money she wants/needs or with the object she was thinking of purchasing. This is downright prostitution inside marriage and, though men can be too naive to acknowledge it, women know and end up by hating themselves and their partner with unpredictable consequences.

Other women marry well-to-do men and gladly give up their jobs. Typically, these women don't seem to be engaged in fulfilling activities but in whatever helps them make ends meet. They find marriage a lucrative exchange in which they give up their freedom of decision, scanty as it may be, for the sake of a life in the lap of luxury. (Perhaps luxury is not part of the real picture, but if they believe it . . .) These women may place themselves into very hard situations. However kind and generous their husbands are, the ghost of "what if" haunts them day and night. "What if he falls in love with someone else?" "What if he gets tired of me?" "What if I don't age well?" If they have signed a pre-nup, these wives can well stretch themselves out like a rug under their husbands' feet to be trodden on for fear of going back where they came from. Unconsciously, sometimes even the kindest men figuratively wipe their boots on such women. I guess it must be quite difficult to resist the temptation when someone seems to be begging you to use them at your will.

Shall we now, in all fairness, take a glance at the other side of the coin? When a married man, particularly if he is a father, loses his job, he may tend to view it as the end of the world, all the more so if he is the household's sole/primary breadwinner. On the one hand, and for reasons worth examining, most men don't seem to be prepared to work at something different from what they've been doing. One could safely argue (sorry to hurt your feelings if you, sir, belong in this category) that, at least in this respect, men have a one-track mind. Many lack resourcefulness to change horses in the middle of the river, and stubbornly pursue the same kind of job they lost. As time passes, they fall into depression, which prevents them to continue their search. If their wives work, or if stay-at-home wives find a way to keep the home together, resentment sets in. The ambivalence discussed in *Living with Stress*, the first volume of this series, explains the contradiction. Supposedly, these men should be grateful that their wives' salaries keep the wolf away from the door. This should encourage them to persist in their endeavors for a new job, but unfortunately the so much bragged of acceptance of role reversal in marriage seems to work much better in writings about gender issues than in real life. The *macho* style—the patriarchal view of the division of labor in the family—is more common than one would imagine. Jobless men depend on their wives' management of money, and don't usually take it kindly. The difference between their predicament and that of women lies in the fact that, culturally, the male collective unconscious has no inscription of economic dependence on women. Thus men in this situation tend to become sullen, to pick unnecessary quarrels, and to feel victimized by society and their wives.

I trust that I have succeeded in making my point in defense of money. However, it is not big money we're talking about. A clever lawyer told me once that as long as I spent all of my time working, none was left "to make money." His point was that the kind of money of, say, the Darlings in *Dirty, Sexy Money* entailed having free time to stay alert for business opportunities, take risks, and not fear dirtying one's hands a little (or a lot) in the process. In fact, it is not precisely one's hands that one dirties, but the metaphor is still valid.

By now you probably have an idea about what you want. Assuming that you have decided that money is not it, it will help you to learn what unconscious mechanisms may lie at the root of your choice. And if you do want money, you need to know what is stalling you. Both stances, believe it or not, are triggered by exactly the same mechanisms.

Before reading on, use the blank page/s at the end of this

part to decide whether you feel that, given certain changes (specify which), you could become a "winner." If you are haunted by the idea that you're a loser, jot down why. And if you can already glean the third position, explain what it means to you. The book will not leave the third position unexplained, but it would be great for you to make an educated guess now and contrast it with the suggested answer when you reach the corresponding section.

1.7

Fantasy and reality

Sholem Aleichem, a Russian writer who, among many other works, wrote a series of stories under the title of *Tevye the Milkman*, inspired the immortal musical *Fiddler on the Roof*, set in a small village at the time when the Tsar had just issued a decree for the eviction of all Jews.

Poor as he was, Tevye still had dreams, best expressed in one of the songs that immortalized both the theater and the film version of the musical. By analyzing a few fragments of the lyrics, we can have a pretty clear idea of what "rich" means to a poor man.

> If I were a rich man,
> Ya ha deedle deedle, bubba bubba deedle deedle dum.
> All day long I'd biddy biddy bum.

Since none of the recorded meanings of "biddy" matches the context, I assume that it should be taken onomatopoeically together with the ending "bum." When words lack denotation or connotation, we are free to provide the meanings that come to our mind. I strongly suspect that "all day long I'd biddy biddy dum" suggests that Tevye would idle around. In his fantasy, and lacking the experience of wealth, he cannot realize that a rich man needs to work very hard indeed if he wants to stay rich. Money and property do not take care of themselves, and no wise man would help himself to his fortune thinking it inexhaustible.

> If I were a wealthy man.
> I wouldn't have to work hard

Here is the confirmation of the assumption made above. In his present state, Tevye imagines that hard work consists in tending to his cows and delivering the milk. He cannot imagine that the rich also fret and work, and that when they don't, they soon fall from the wealthy status they enjoyed, with the additional disadvantage that they don't know how to manage on an exceedingly slender budget.

> I'd build a big tall house with rooms by the dozen,
> Right in the middle of the town.
> A fine tin roof with real wooden floors below.
> There would be one long staircase just going up,
> And one even longer coming down,
> And one more leading nowhere, just for show.

"Just for show." Together with the coming lines "For the town to see and hear," our poor man feels that the whole point of wealth lies in flaunting it. What satisfaction could be derived from having money if no one knows how well you have done in life? Tevye probably thinks that his neighbors will admire his coming up in the world, but I wonder whether deep down he doesn't harbor the desire to arouse envy. In *Improving Personal Relationships*, I wrote at length about the real significance and consequences of envy. When you awaken this poisonous snake, you will be bitten sooner rather than later. Tevye, a simple man, may not be aware of this. However, one would have expected him to be familiar with an old Jewish curse: "May you be the richest man in your family." Does it surprise you that such a kind-sounding phrase is, in fact, a curse? The richest man will be envied, harassed with requests for money, flattered and lied to by his relatives, who behaving thus hope that some or all of his money will find its way to their own pockets and, which seems the worst picture, hesitating about who to trust, will finally trust no one.

Sensible rich people tend to indulge themselves in a rather quiet way. They talk about money while doing business or in the company of their equals. The less "the other half" knows about their actual wealth the better. They have nothing to prove, even if they take pride in having amassed their own fortune. In many cases, when the sick need for control and/or the thirst for power doesn't prey on their minds, at some point—and sometimes even before reaching this point—the rich decide that they have enough to last them many lives over, and engage in helping/sponsoring a number of deserving others. They do this quietly too, because they're not seeking either publicity or praise.

I'd fill my yard with chicks and turkeys and geese
    and ducks
For the town to see and hear.
And each loud "cheep" and "squawk" and "honk"
    and "quack"
Would land like a trumpet on the ear,
As if to say "Here lives a wealthy man."

The above stanza reinforces the notion of "just for show." It would be great if Tevye wished to fill his yard with poultry in order to serve the community, not necessarily through charity, but through business. Yet in his conception of wealth, the poultry amounts to the gold or silver tableware that a poor man of the city, for instance, would desire as a mark of wealth. I understand that someone who has been struggling against poverty from birth and who has had to put up with the snubs of the better off in his village may well entertain these thoughts. However, they lead nowhere except to some buried feeling of revenge for the humiliation so long endured. It is true that revenge may act as a powerful motor toward wealth. But the lingering bitterness prevents the now rich man from fully enjoying his newly acquired fortune. It would seem as if all economic success accompanied by negative mindsets boomeranged badly against the achievers.

I see my wife, my Golde, looking like a rich man's wife
With a proper double-chin.
Supervising meals to her heart's delight.

I see her putting on airs and strutting like a peacock.
Oy, what a happy mood she's in.
Screaming at the servants, day and night.

Tevye's wife is aptly named "Golde," the Yiddish for "gold."
The poor man equates richness to fatness (the "proper double-chin"). In those days, many rich ladies, if not actually fat, were definitely stout or plump. In our times, things work differently. Obesity or overweight is a disease of the poor, who survive on an excess of fats and carbohydrates combined with sugar. The rich tend to keep slim, for the simple reason that they can afford a different, healthier kind of food. Still, Tevye was right to dream of a fleshy wife, for by the standards of his society fatness pointed to prosperity. What makes me wonder once again about his fantasies is his joy at seeing Golde "putting on airs and strutting like a peacock," the best known verbal representations of vanity. What good is it to be rich if you don't behave in the way you suppose the rich do? And, more disturbing, ill-treating the servants would make her happy! I agree that a number of rich people have no consideration at all for their servants. But this isn't because of their wealth but because of their nature, their upbringing, or both. There goes another gross misconception of a trait attached to money.

The most important men in town would come to fawn
    on me!
They would ask me to advise them,
Like a Solomon the Wise.
"If you please, Reb Tevye . . ."

"Pardon me, Reb Tevye . . ."
Posing problems that would cross a rabbi's eyes!
And it won't make one bit of difference if I answer
    right or wrong.
When you're rich, they think you really know!

The last two lines are hair-raising, since so many poor people sincerely believe that the rich know better. That is to say, if they knew how to grow rich (we need to leave aside heirs of huge estates), it must mean that they know everything else. Nothing could be farther from the truth. Knowledge and money do not necessarily go hand in hand. You can probably have better access to knowledge through the proper use of money, but ultimately lots of brains prove disastrous when it comes to money issues.

Aleichem never intended to depict a fool. Among other things, his Tevye stories satirically illustrate a most unfair world in which, at times, fantasy is so far removed from reality that it needs to create a reality of its own to avoid madness and, at other times, fantasy and reality blend in such a way that one cannot tell them apart.

Now, in which of these realms do *you* live? Use the blank pages at the end of this part to write down your fantasies about the rich and what you would do if you were a rich man.

The picture of a poor man's fantasies about wealth described above is not universal. The upper middle class and the rich have built their own fantasies about how the poor view money. In their conception, and because they revere wealth, the poor entertain totally mistaken ideas about the lives of those who are rolling in money. A great example of this is O'Henry's short story *While the Auto Waits*, in which a wealthy young aristocrat taking a walk in the park passes himself off as a member of the lower classes while a cashier pretends to belong in the elite. She never gets to know who he really is, but a slip, the product of her fantasies, gives her away.

See how the dialogue goes:

"I wanted to talk, for once, with a natural man—one unspoiled by the despicable gloss of wealth and supposed social superiority. Oh! you do not know how weary I am of it—money, money, money! And of the men who surround me, dancing like little marionettes all cut by the same pattern. I am sick of pleasure, of jewels, of travel, of society, of luxuries of all kinds."

"I always had an idea," ventured the young man, hesitatingly, "that money must be a pretty good thing."

"A competence is to be desired. But when you have so many millions that—!" She concluded the sentence with a gesture of despair. "It is the monotony of it" she continued, "that palls. Drives, dinners, theatres, balls, suppers, with the gilding of superfluous wealth over it all. Sometimes the very tinkle of the ice in my champagne glass nearly drives me mad." [. . .] "at a dinner party this week on Madison Avenue a green kid glove was laid by the plate of each guest to be put on and used while eating olives."

Ice cubes in the champagne and green kid gloves to eat olives proved a little too much. Unlike Tevye, the cashier does not fantasize about what she would do if she were rich but about how the rich live. And she got it all wrong, apart from the fact that she probably missed the opportunity for a romantic liaison that might have made her rich, for the young aristocrat was genuinely interested in her until she overdid it. He wouldn't have minded her being poor, but would not put up with what he viewed as snobbery. The sad thing is that, far from being a snob, the poor girl (both meanings attached) was only giving free rein to her imagination.

Late Argentine economist and writer Enrique Silberstein speaks of reality in the bond between the poor and money. He declares that the poor have never respected money, insofar as the money that reaches them comes in the form of small bills discarded by the rich, and that there is no time for a connection between the object "money" and the poor because no sooner do the poor lay hands on money than they have to let go of it to pay debts or buy essentials. "There is no contact or relation between the poor and money."*

If this is true—Silberstein grounds his assertions on the fact that in the race between the poor v. money, the latter always wins by a head, and on the slang that somehow deprives money of its halo—one could conclude that the poor are happy to stay poor. Alternately, one could also conclude that "the grapes are sour." Is this what is hindering you from giving moneymaking your best shot? You're probably not poor. Still, perhaps you believe that you share with them the curse of your hard-earned money taking

---

* Enrique Silberstein. *El hombre ante la riqueza*, in Janus 9.

flight to pay endless bills with none sticking to your hand. Someone once said to me, "Money is like a tennis ball that goes from one side of the court to the other as I watch without the slightest chance of holding it for a moment." Give some thought to this. If you're convinced from the start that you and money are just not made for each other, you will not make any, no matter how hard you want to. Positive thinking, as explained in *Living with Stress*, is the first step out of a pessimistic outlook.

Fiction literature and movies abound in stories that develop dreams of wealth. *The Apprenticeship of Duddy Kravitz*, a novel by Mordecai Richler later made into a film, tells the story of a poor Quebec boy raised in an environment that fills his head with a quasi-religious worship of power and money. His ruling mandate is his grandfather's motto—"A man without land is a nobody"—and Duddy accordingly plans his route toward success with this goal in mind. His path is devious, sometimes openly dishonest and others brushing on dishonesty. His blindness to human connections outside those that can aid his ambition turn him into a selfish, uncaring man, for he seems to have pledged his vows to Mammon. What can be said for this character is that not once did he waver along the thorny way to wealth, and that all that talk about money pouring into his ears from men who felt they were "nobody" because they hadn't become rich was bound to leave an unerasable imprint on his mind. Duddy consciously renounced the blessings of love and friendship for the sake of a choice that, not being his own at the beginning, eventually became very much his decision.

This is an example of how our surroundings can permanently affect our lives. If Duddy's father, relatives, neighbors, and teachers hadn't tried to vicariously change their "loser" status through Duddy's endeavors which, in their imaginary, reached out to all of them, perhaps he would have led a more fulfilling emotional life with a little less money. Or perhaps not. As the saying goes, if "ifs" and "ands" were pots and pans, there'd be no work for tinkers.

Wall Street, a 1987 Oliver Stone release featuring Michael Douglas and Charlie Sheen, shows a different kind of reaction to family values. Bud (Charlie Sheen) is a young man who simply cannot accept his father Carl's (Martin Sheen) dull conformism to a monotonous life of low wages and self-sacrifice. Carl has worked his way up to the top (i.e., his roof) and is now maintenance chief with a small airline company. He would have liked Bud to join him, but the youngster hated the lack of horizons, the cheap food and clothes, the suburbia and, above all, the idea that there was a roof to ambition. He goes into stockbroking, bends over backward to do business with Gekko, a ruthless, shady Wall Street shark, and at some point realizes that his golden dream will inevitably bring about the downfall of the airline company, leaving his father and the rest of the workers in the street. At the last minute, Bud takes his father's side, turns Gekko over to the police and agrees that he too deserves punishment for the illegal financial maneuvers in which he participated.

Again, the set of values that a father laboriously taught, mostly by setting the example, yielded fruit in the nick of time. It all goes to show that those early experiences mentioned in the introduction may lie dormant in the psyche until some conjuncture sets them in motion.

You may wonder why these two cases, like many others in the realm of entertainment, do not have a happy ending. Well, it has nothing to do with money, but with morality. It wouldn't look right to allow people with ill-gotten gains walk scot-free and enjoy their wealth. In real life, things tend to work differently. Many large fortunes over the world were started through either downright illegal or morally questionable means to be "cleansed" by later generations. In a way, Michael Corleone (*The Godfather* trilogy) expected to shift to legal business during his lifetime, but the spiderweb he got caught into snatched his daughter's life. The Corleone family, though a literary creation by Mario Puzo, sums up a number of real people that drew the author's attention as he was doing research for the novel.

Although Puzo focused on the Mob's organization and ties with the political power, other traditional, enormously wealthy families may have been very careful to conceal the hazy origins of their fortune. Through lack of evidence, these rumors (we need to dub them so, precisely because they cannot be proved) have been dismissed as "urban legends." However, a phrase that our ineffable humorist Quino put in the lips of his character Mafalda keeps haunting my mind: "You cannot amass a fortune without grinding others into flour."

No truth is absolute. It does, however, strike our attention that the best-known literature dealing with moneymaking seats on a base of corruption. If one accepts that, as from approximately the 1940s, fiction took a centripetal turn to focus on the individual rather than on the society, one should also accept that, from a literary point of view, it's not at all interesting to devise narratives of spotless people. This had already been understood by 19th century writers like Balzac, many of whose characters had a nasty moral squint where money was concerned.

You know of the complaints against certain video games, TV programs, magazines, and books based on allegations that they encourage criminal behavior. You also know that it takes a lot more than fantasy to enact unlawful deeds. Still, perhaps the flood of corruption gushing out from the media and from fictional works causes you to rebel against money, the beginning and end of corruption. "I am not like that!" your mind screams, and you go to such extents to preserve your moral integrity that you overlook perfectly legitimate opportunities of improving your economic standing.

The trouble seems to be that the boundaries between right and wrong have become somewhat blurred. Practices that were unthinkable in the past (for example, bribing a company executive to learn about your competitors before entering a bid for a contract) now appear as part of a regular negotiation. In a case like this, the bribe may be hinted at by the executive herself, or insinuated by the interested party. Money is not mentioned in the exchange. But as long as either of the people involved says something as vague as "a cruise to the Bahamas," the bottomline is still money. Please use the blank page/s at the end of this section to list practices involving money that you find questionable.

MY VIEWS ON THE UNDERSIDE OF MONEY

I COULD MAKE MONEY IF . . .

I WILL NEVER MAKE MONEY BECAUSE . . .

I UNDERSTAND THAT THE THIRD POSITION MIGHT BE . . .

MY FANTASIES ABOUT THE RICH

WHAT WOULD I DO IF I WERE A RICH MAN?

PRACTICES THAT I FIND QUESTIONABLE

2

2.1

The effects of the unconscious

As has been said in the introduction, your early experiences related to money or to the sundry aspects of life it symbolizes may have shaped your present predicament. In Part 1 you read that, in principle, there should be no reason for your rejecting the effort money implies. The connection between both ideas is that reasons related to your infancy and blocked from your conscious mind may result in a negative outcome in regard to money.

The unconscious guides most, if not all, of our decisions. I know how hard it must be to accept that your carefully thought-out steps concerning choice of career, marriage, money making and others respond to something that has no visible location in the body. However, if you have read *Living with Stress* and *Improving Personal Relationships*, you already know that the unconscious can be made conscious through the so-called formations of the unconscious and through introspection or the practice of Neuro-linguistic Programming (NLP). The difference between the former and the latter ways resides in the fact that the formations of the unconscious are spontaneous, since it's not up to you to decide what will come to you in your sleep (dreams) and your slips of the tongue are certainly not intentional, while introspection and NLP are voluntary actions to bring unconscious aspects to light. Of course, psychoanalysis pursues the same end, but as it involves someone else's professional work, it lies beyond the scope of self-help.

The other two books in this series have provided you with a clue to the construction of the subject. You need to remember that the course of our lives is not predetermined from birth, and that once the subject emerges with all its components, it does so with a structure that results partly from genetic predisposition and partly from nurture. Please do not think that genetic predisposition applies in every case. It is generally agreed that it may constitute a factor in schizophrenia and depression, but you cannot blame your genes for your inability to make money. The structure, once established, will not change. What can change is your attitude to it. In other words, you can make the best of your structure by handling it to your advantage provided that you know what hinders you from achieving your goals.

You may remember that Transactional Analysis poses that we are "recording machines" that store everything that happens and is said to us and around us from our earliest days.

In such a context, the stories that you're about to read intend to show you that your perception of parental behavior may have wrecking consequences for your relation to money.

Recapitulating the main problems recorded as stemming from childhood experiences will enable you to create a link between them and others whose origin is perhaps less clear. In addition, a closer view of the intrapsychic processes mentioned and their bearing on real life may provide answers to your own queries.

Let us peep into the lives of real people who might well have gone through the same as many readers. I will outline five leading cases and point to a number of considerations that may have led the characters away from the psychic possibility of making money (and keeping it.)

2.2

Kevin Culley was born to a couple in which the father's role consisted in managing and increasing his inherited wealth while the mother devised ways of spending money for the whole family to enjoy the very best that the market offered. Mr. Culley used to keep late hours. After a perfunctory exchange with the housekeeper, Mrs. Culley was off to the beauty parlor, the body fitness center, lunch with friends, you name it. Husband and wife spent their evenings at social gatherings, the theater, the opera, or else threw parties at home. Kevin was raised by a first-class nanny until he was old enough to attend kindergarten and then school, which filled his day with curricular and extracurricular activities besides providing him with the seeds of the social life he was expected to have as a teenager of the privileged class.

When you're not familiar with lifestyles different from your own, you tend to think that yours is everyone else's as well. Kevin's parents rarely shared quality time (or just time) with him, but they showered him with toys and state-of-the art gadgets and, when the time was right, gave him a great car and a generous allowance for which he didn't have to account. If you had asked him how he felt back then, he would have told you that he didn't have a care in the world.

Ever since his birth the Culleys took for granted that Kevin would major in Business Administration to work side by side with his father in the company and take over from him on Mr. Culley's retirement. The youngster never objected to this until, to his utter surprise, he discovered that in the last year of secondary school he was becoming more and more interested in music than in numbers. That he wanted to devote his future to music came to him as a revelation that brought on a severe shock to his parents. After a harsh lecture by Mr. Culley, with Mrs. Culley quietly nodding from a recently purchased designer couch, Kevin was ordered to forget "all that nonsense" and do his duty to the family. In order to make it clear that he was not an insensitive man, his father told him that he had felt attracted to painting at Kevin's age ("And I was really good at it, mind you; my art teacher thought I had a great career ahead of me") but that fortunately his own father had put some sense into his head. "Are you aware of the kind of life that awaits you?" had asked his father. "Can you picture yourself waiting tables while the 'great career' materializes, supposing it does? For let me tell you that if you abandon the family; that is to say, if you refuse to keep the company going as I did when the responsibility fell on me, the family will abandon you. Freedom of choice comes with a price. You're welcome to enjoy the proverbial poverty of the artist." Kevin's father laughed at the memory. "It's normal for youth and lack of practicality to join hands. Look, I know you hate us right now. But you'll hate us even more if we let you stray from your legitimate place in society. Here, let's enhance your allowance a little to sugar a bitter pill to swallow." And he produced his checkbook, wrote out a huge check and handed it to Kevin as he winked his eye at Mrs. Culley. "Oh my," he exclaimed. "We're already late for the fund raiser. Bye, son. We'll be talking again soon."

Frenzied flashes of broken thoughts cascaded into Kevin's mind. They could be summarized into the completely new realization that money and what money could buy had parented and nurtured him. His diapers had been changed by paid help, he had sucked at his bottle held by paid arms (Mrs. Culley had not breast-fed him), wiled away his idle hours with extravagant toys; his whole life had been organized and structured by money. Mother and Father were emotionally dried up trees whose only daily yield was money, and the same could be said of his friends' parents.

He recalled the time when he had fallen off his bike and got a nasty cut on his forehead. The housekeeper had driven him to hospital and brought him back home with a couple of stitches. When his mother arrived home, she remarked he'd been lucky the accident hadn't had really serious consequences and sent for a new computer game so that he kept his mind busy with something he enjoyed. He recalled that his mixed curiosity and anxiety about sex were (poorly, and probably mistakenly) resolved through pamphlets and conversations with other kids who knew as little as he did, for his father stalled a "man to man" conversation for "the right time, which isn't now, with the stock market worrying me to death." Still, just to help him out,

Mr. Culley had given him a few tips on how to look for a reliable escort service—that's what he called it—and told him to charge the cost to his credit card. Every memory ended in more or less the same way.

Kevin came to the conclusion that money turned people into shadows thirsting for more money, that they never had enough, and that not an ounce of genuine human feeling—the kind of feeling that he had read about in the prescribed books at school and that arose in him when he listened to the lyrics of his favorite musicians—stood the slightest chance of piercing the money barrier. He dutifully graduated from High School, didn't send in his applications to Business School, said nothing at his parents' offer of a tour of Europe before "starting the really hard work," as Mr. Culley put it, quietly packed a couple of T-shirts, jeans, and sweaters, gave a big parting hug to the housekeeper, left a laconic note and the epiphanic check under a Lalique lamp on his mother's bedside table, and hit the road with the three hundred dollars he had earned writing papers for lazy or ungifted schoolmates.

The youth thumbed his way to San Francisco, experienced hardships and dangerous situations, toiled at jobs he didn't even know existed, perfected his skills at the guitar and eventually became a tolerably good performer. However, he kept changing bands, for as soon as the one he was in began making good money, he quit to join some unknown group or played solo for relatively low pay. His reasons to quit never involved money issues . . . consciously. Kevin married an average singer whose ambitions didn't go further than a small apartment in an inexpensive district, and the couple had two girls who saw luxury only in films but enjoyed parental closeness and undivided attention. Cut off from the family source of income, quite often Kevin did want big money, money earned with his own talent, especially for the sake of the girls, and complained that he just didn't seem to possess the shrewd business ability that drove a number of his fellow musicians to the best paid status of their activity, including ownership of music companies.

If your case resembles Kevin's in whole or in part, you need to know that, just as in other stories that you will read later, he unconsciously shifted the cause of his uneasiness from his parents, whom he loved despite appearances to the contrary, to the inanimate object money, which he could hate without misgivings or remorse. Why do I say that he loved his parents? Because I've told you the facts from Kevin's point of view, as he reasoned them in his conscious mind. Among the unconscious processes that took place, at least two stand out and deserve analysis. One is that a child's need to feel loved and to love in return is such that even physically or psychically abused children either blame themselves or resort to denial in order to establish an imaginary love bond with their parents. The other is the selectivity of memory. The check incident, which I will call trauma although it does not strictly respond to the standard definition, triggered a chain of associations that reinforced Kevin's feelings of frustration at that moment while blocking other memories that would have contradicted the absoluteness of his judgement. All truth is relative and subjective, there's no "whole" truth in terms of human behavior, and every participant in an event will tell her version, the one she genuinely believes is "the truth." Moreover, one same participant will volunteer a different narrative at a different time. Still, our Kevin, because of his personality traits, deliberately avoided finding himself in a winning position out of an unconscious fear of reliving the trauma.

Seen from the outside, and without putting on paper other possible factors in the narration, it seems that the Culleys substituted money for explicit parental warmth. However, by believing that his parents' attitude to him had somehow been shaped by money, Kevin inverted the terms of the problem, which is an acceptable defense mechanism in childhood but a sad misinterpretation in adulthood. The kernel of the first story is that Kevin perceived money as something dehumanizing and evil because, in his view, his parents substituted money for human warmth, manifest love, and caregiving. The importance of the phrase "in his view" cannot be overemphasized. All throughout this series you've been warned that, when you get down to brass tacks, perception is the key. Perhaps Kevin's parents did exactly this and perhaps not. And even if they did, in all probability they didn't mean harm, though it would take a lengthy analysis of their circumstances to determine why they raised their child in this way. The motives underlying Mr. Culley's line of conduct seem to have been dictated by his own father's attitude to him; the reasons that drove Mrs. Culley to go along remain open to speculation. Notice that Mr. Culley, forced to dismiss the idea of a career in art by a father who felt it his right to shape his son's life, became a rich, successful businessman *like* his father. Therefore, he must have thought that verbally roughing up Kevin a little would produce a similar effect. Parents generally tend to either do onto their children as their own parents did onto them, or do exactly the opposite if they feel unhappy at the outcome. They rarely think of the third position, a concept I mentioned in Part 1 and that will still remain pending in regard to money. Here the third position means producing new behavior, adopting grandparental positive aspects *and* taking into account that the child is nobody's clone, but a new, different individual.

So, again, if you recognize yourself in Kevin, go to the blank pages at the end of this part and answer truthfully the questions you will find there.

Sayings like "the apple doesn't fall far from the tree" or "a chip off the old block" are not oracular. With the help of the questionnaire, your introspection may change your impossibility of making money and return you to a world in which money, having lost its psychological overtones as it should, is just a necessary tool of trade.

2.3

The youngest of three siblings, Stella Wilkins literally spent her time at home in early childhood stopping her ears to keep out the yelling. Her brothers seemed to have got used to it and went about their homework or games as if the terrifying scenes between their parents were just background noise. The rows were always about money. They invariably started at breakfast, with Mrs. Wilkins, a stay-at-home mom, asking Mr. Wilkins to buy something that he said they couldn't afford. He argued that they were already heavily indebted with their credit card company, and that she should manage to live within their means. This never failed to infuriate his wife, who screamed an endless list of reproaches at him. "If you made more money we wouldn't be stuck with this impossible dishwasher! It so embarrasses me to lie about where we go on vacation!" and she rattled on and on until Mr. Wilkins exploded and yelled back at her that she was a lousy administrator, had all her priorities wrong, and it wasn't as if they were living in a shack. With variations, these scenes took place at least twice a day. When Mr. Wilkins was at work and the children at home, Mrs. Wilkins poured their father's inability to give them "a decent life" into their ears. She also vented her regrets for quitting her job at the company she worked for when she first became pregnant. "I could have reached the top and earned a lot more than your father ever will," she half sighed, half grunted.

If anything, things grew worse as time passed. Eventually Stella graduated as a clothes designer and got a job at a small, innovative firm that valued her ideas about fashion. In fact, the firm made headway thanks to her creativity. But she never demanded to be paid more than she was offered, and it made her uncomfortable when her friends insisted that she not only deserved a handsome salary and participation in the profits (which she wasn't being given) but also some kind of partnership.

Thus Stella lived on an adequate income, but couldn't fight for her economic rights, just as she couldn't think of looking for a better position and concomitant perks somewhere else. The clothing habits in Asian and African countries she had read of had inspired many of her designs, and she longed to experience life in such countries. This implied having money to spare, money that Stella wanted badly but couldn't bring herself to get. "What's wrong with me?" she wondered. "Why can't I take the bull by the horns and do what I know is right?" Her answer to the inner voice that tortured her with these questions was that, like her father, she obviously wasn't cut out to make money. Perhaps if she had taken after her mother . . .

What Stella didn't know was that when a couple's bone of contention is money, the problem usually lies somewhere else. Deep down, and often unconsciously, the partners feel that tackling the real issues will put an end to the marriage. With the ambivalence that tends to accompany human behavior, they probably would like to call off the relationship but also fear making a mistake that may ruin their lives, particularly if no third party is involved. It cannot be overlooked that dissatisfaction raises its head in fuelling these quarrels, but it's a "hydra-head." One or both partners have become disappointed in the other, the sex is not good, some emotional voids that they expected the other to fill remain empty, the attractive person they fell in love with turned out to be boring/thoughtless/selfish. . . . Yet unless yours is a mature relationship in which everything can be calmly discussed with a view to find a solution that works for both, once you have told your partner to her face how you truly feel about whatever is gnawing at you there's no turning back. The accumulated bitterness will make the one who speaks out first choose the worst words, those that hurt the other beyond repair. Unconscious awareness of this opens up the money department, in which each partner feels it safe to give free rein to her anger and frustration without brushing on the real, personal grudges.

It seems clear from the example that Mrs. Wilkins would have preferred to keep her job, not because of the money, but because she would have been "somebody" in other people's eyes and, most importantly, in her own. We don't know about her other frustrations, but we can speculate that if Mr. Wilkins had performed amazingly in bed, she wouldn't have focused so hard on the dishwasher.

You may be thinking that Stella's family life should have driven her to *make money* so that a) she could avoid the suffering that her mother was exposed to and, b) gain access to the things she wanted. What you're not taking into account—and neither was Stella, that's why she gave herself the wrong answers—is the matter of identification.

There's no rough and ready way to explain this complex process. Quoting Laplanche and Pontalis in my own translation, it is "a psychological process through which a subject assimilates some aspect or characteristic of another subject and uses it as a model for her own partial or total construction. Personality becomes constituted and differentiated through a series of identifications." Simplifying a little (a lot, I dare say, but we need to bear in mind once again that this series is not a treatise on psychoanalysis), Stella identified with her father and her adult behavior was consistent with maintaining this identification. Perhaps because Mr. Wilkins appeared as the weakest party in the couple, her psyche was drawn to what the patriarchal society we still live in calls "the feminine position." Furthermore, it has proved quite rare that, without some kind of professional aid, a subject may find the courage to surpass or go farther than the parental figure she has identified with. The unconscious seems to set a boundary in order to preserve the model, which would amount to protect the subject as it was constructed.

The main point in this story is that Stella failed to make money not because to her it symbolized "evil" but because she (unconsciously, of course; all identifications are unconscious processes) identified with her economically unsuccessful father. The extent to which he was unsuccessful is debatable. As he said, "it wasn't as if they were living in a shack." In spite of Mrs. Wilkins's complaints, their home seemed to have the essential laborsaving devices, even if a state-of-the-art dishwasher wasn't affordable. (By the way, such a one would be upwards of $1000.) And they did go away on vacation, though not to the exotic or fashionable places Mrs. Wilkins would have loved to brag of. You read that, in a couple, most quarrels involving money or the objects that money can buy conceal some other kind of trouble or dissatisfaction. One was proposed as a possible cause of Mrs. Wilkins's bitterness, but we could include others. The accusations that her husband leveled at her about being a lousy administrator and having her priorities wrong may have been well grounded. If so, Mrs. Wilkins squandered the family budget (remember the debts to the credit card companies), probably because her imaginary differed widely from her husband's. She sounds like a "keep-up-with-the-Joneses" type, a status lover, understanding status as the possession of market-value goods.

On the other hand, we don't know that Mr. Wilkins ever went the extra mile to make the kind of money that it takes to live the golden life. This isn't an assumption, since he never said anything like "I do my best, but . . ." The dotted line stands for whatever explained his impossibility to make more money. We then conclude that Mr. Wilkins didn't want to move up the money ladder for reasons that escape us. Right at the beginning of this book, I told you that it was a perfectly legitimate decision insofar as you were not living off others. What happens when you're not living off others but depriving others of things they want badly? It all depends on who those others are (their role in your family structure) and on what they demand. If we're talking about your children, it's only fair to give them what other children at your same economic level have. Yet it's a big mistake to give them more than that. Your money should constitute a solid base for your children to develop their capacities without having to worry about sudden eviction, for example. But if you encourage them to play the "mine is better than yours" game, you're teaching them to compete for a shallow purpose, to put it mildly. The prize of this game is peer jealousy. Sooner or later, some other child will appear with a more expensive object, and then your child will demand something else, with the moon as a limit. How healthy can this be? Moreover, you may have destined the money to something you need/want. If you postpone your own needs/likes to give your child something extravagant and unnecessary, what she will read between the lines is that you don't value yourself enough to get *your* priorities right. As value and respect are synonyms in this context, you're not entitled to her respect unless you respect yourself. These behaviors are also triggered by unconscious mechanisms related to low parental self-esteem. Parents with a deficit in narcissism will act wisely if they acknowledge the problem and work on it, for in the long run their offspring may react "ungratefully" (this is what parents say) without the parents ever realizing what went wrong in the first place.

Now, if the "other" is a spouse, think of the issues at stake. Your spouse may prompt you to make more money because she knows you have the stamina and your effort will make everyone happy, including you. Our Mrs. Wilkins definitely didn't belong in this category. She was all about "I," and tried to turn her children into active allies by demeaning their father. Even when the boys didn't seem to pay much attention, they must have felt affected by these quarrels. On her part, Stella was seriously upset, probably because of her identification with her father and because she also loved her mother. Mr. Wilkins stood his ground and fought back and, from what we know, he spared the children the suffering of having to take sides. Why this couple stayed together is anybody's guess. One might speculate that money played a part in the decision, at least as far as Mrs. Wilkins was concerned. Cut off from the job market, her lifestyle would have changed for the worse, no matter how good a settlement she might have got during the divorce proceedings.

It is worth noting that Stella's model, the one that her unconscious picked for identification, shouldn't be understood as "my father who cannot make enough money to please my mother." There must have been other traits in the model that were "attracted" to shape the process. Under different circumstances, since no two identification processes are the same, her unconscious might have left out this particular trait. However, perhaps because she perceived Mr. Wilkins's shortcomings in this respect as a salient characteristic thanks to her mother's constant attacks, that aspect of the model took on an outsized dimension in the package.

Lastly, I mentioned in passing the impossibility of going farther than has the parental figure with which the subject identifies. Among other deterring mechanisms, fear and love play a major part in this, though not concurrently. Supposing the internalized parent arouses feelings of fear in the subject, she will "defend" herself from the imaginary anger this figure might throw at her by unconsciously flying, so to speak, under the radar. This leaves the internalized parent at an advantage, thus giving her no reason to inflict punishment on the subject. It doesn't really matter whether the parent is dead or alive. Because past, present, and future blend in the unconscious (that is to say, to all practical purposes everything is present), the subject will behave as if the internalized parent were alive and strong enough to take revenge for the subject having dared achieved more. In Stella's case, identification love prevented her to surpass her (internalized) father, for she would have felt guilty of inflicting him an imaginary wound to top the humiliation she perceived he must have suffered as her mother nagged him on his inadequacy. In her conscious life, Stella went only as far as her father did, not because she rejected money, but because she unconsciously protected her identification model from further debasement.

If you recognize aspects of yourself in the Stella character, go to the blank pages at the end of this chapter and answer truthfully the questions there. You will find that it's possible to rid yourself from the harmful traits of a model you didn't even know you had picked. You will then make money or not, but at least it will depend entirely on you and not on childhood fixations.

2.4

Thirteen-year-old Dimitri Vassilias, born in Salonika, and his slightly elder brother were put on a United States–bound boat in the early 20th century. The Balkan wars had left an aftermath of instability that depleted their parents' hope for better times. They felt too old to start a new life at the other end of the world, but their staunch nature inspired them not to tie their sons to a future without horizons. The boys were more or less trained in the family trade (furniture carving), and they had distant relatives in New York who had set up a small business and who agreed to take in the children and see to their well being.

As it turned out, the New York based Vassiliases were more interested in getting cheap labor than in giving the children a proper education. The brothers slept on thin mattresses on the workshop floor, worked from dawn to dusk, and picked up the language mostly from American workers and occasional street acquaintances. However, they were keen on learning as much as they could about every aspect of the business. At 18, after a heated argument with his would-be uncle, who refused to promote them to a better position or to improve their living conditions, Dimitri grabbed his elder yet less ambitious brother by the arm and stalked out of the workshop, determined to open a furniture company of his own. He went to the richest Greek businessman in the city and spent days at his door, until Mr. Karidis agreed to listen to him ("You have five minutes. Start counting.") just to get him out of his hair.

Dimitri laid out a brilliant business plan on Mr. Karidis's table, and the old gentleman, who was no fool, realized that it would bring him much more money than his present undertakings did. After drawing a fair contract with the brothers, he provided them with the means to get started. To cut a long story short, the Vassilias brothers succeeded in capturing the market through vision, dedication, and hard work. The elder, to his brother's utter disapproval, married young. Dimitri objected that you couldn't take good care of a family and a business in the making at the same time, and that sooner or later one would suffer. At thirty-six, he himself began looking for a suitable wife once the company was firmly established, and married Fatima, a ravishing girl of Turkish descent—the ironies of life—eighteen years his junior.

They had four children, two girls and two boys, who were taught from day one to respect education (the education that Dimitri had been deprived of) and money. Perhaps it should be said that, under his Western patina, Dimitri had not foregone his ancestral view of the genders, and that Fatima, who came from an impoverished family and thoroughly enjoyed the luxuries lavished on her by her husband, would not dream of contradicting him. Thus the girls went to college, forewarned that they were expected to marry wealthy men not "slut around the professional milieu," and the boys took up Economics and Law respectively, for they would eventually manage the company.

None of these children ever contested their father's decisions. But see what happened. Halfway through the School of Architecture (her father's choice, a becoming ornament for a woman) the elder daughter secretly started dating a nobody—a salesman she met during a shopping spree—and got pregnant by him. She went to her mother for advice, for advice about how to face her father, that is, for she was in love and her boyfriend insisted on marrying her, whether because he too was in love or because he saw the opportunity of changing his fortunes we'll never know. Acknowledged with the facts, Dimitri heavily cursed in Greek and arranged the wedding. But the young salesman never earned his way into the family, for he was run over by a truck and died before the baby was born. His widow was offered an honorable comeback to the parental home, which she refused on the grounds that it would mean falling back under Daddy's thumb. She'd much rather make a living by herself. She managed with very little help, working at sundry jobs until she graduated and was engaged by a large architecture studio. From then on she lived passably well, but never made money. Her projects in that respect were systematically obstructed by external factors (the child fell ill, the currency became devalued, a prospective partner withdrew her support, and so on). When her daughter turned 16, she married another nobody—this time a laboratory technician.

The second daughter took up Medicine. Dimitri was elated; the difficulties posed by the course of studies and his child's ability to overcome them spoke of her superior intelligence. She managed to evade romantic commitment under the pretext that you couldn't study and be distracted by love at the same time (an echo of Dimitri's objections to his brother getting married when he did). Yet when she graduated with honors and her father began pressing her to look around for Mr. Right, she announced that she wasn't particularly attracted to the idea, and that she had accepted an appointment at a hospital in a distant province. She never married, and lived on her salary even after her parents' death, for the company was sold and she donated her share of the proceeds to various children's and old people's homes. The curious thing is that she had mixed feelings about her decision, for on the one hand she felt she was on the earth to fulfill some kind of mission while on the other she kept repeating, "Had I chosen differently, I wouldn't have lost the luxuries that were my daily bread in the city."

The younger son became a lawyer but developed an interest in philosophy that severely estranged him from his father. He wanted nothing with the family business, and Dimitri found some consolation in the fact that it looked *chic* for a wealthy family to boast of an intellectual. What bothered him was that the new-fangled philosopher wouldn't accept economic help. He understood better when his son declared himself a Communist involved in the struggle against Capitalism. Obviously, money was the weapon of the enemy, and its effect on the young man was like that of Kryptonite on Superman. He died young of a disease that money could have cured.

The most intriguing case is that of the elder son. He admired his father, breathed his words of (financial) wisdom, did great work for the company and, at a certain moment, told Dimitri that he wanted to set up in business as an independent entrepreneur without neglecting his duties at the family firm. Generously, Dimitri told him that he had done enough, relieved him from his duties and encouraged him to start whatever business he chose, with his blessings and the initial capital he named.

This son successively tried his luck at four different undertakings, made a fortune every time, and went bankrupt every time as well. He had an incredible ability to make money that was only matched by his ability to lose it. It seemed as if, suddenly, his sense of timeliness got clouded, and while the "off" spell lasted, he took one wrong decision after another. When he came back to his senses, the money was gone, debts were piling up, and he spent months, sometimes years, negotiating with creditors and banks. He's still at it, hoping against hope that he'll succeed in building fortune number five.

One cannot but wonder why none of these sons and daughters followed into their father's footsteps. Their memories don't include neglect like Kevin's or anguishing scenes like Stella's. Identification with the mother doesn't offer a satisfactory explanation, since the mother was the happiest of wives and adored her children. Perhaps we can find a clue in the phrase "the happiest of wives." Often pulling at one tiny end of the skein will unravel the yarn.

For starters, this particular wife unconditionally seconded her husband. She had no will of her own, no desires of her own, not because she acted like a puppet, but because he anticipated her every thought. If the romanticized idea of the perfect husband ever took entity, it was embodied by Dimitri Vassilias. Fatima worshipped him as if he were God, and even though she sometimes felt that he kept the children on a very short leash (yet she dismissed this feeling before it managed to take concrete shape, for how can God be wrong?), she never interfered, following the unwritten patriarchal rule that authority belongs to men.

Two related phenomena occur in early infancy. Freud and Melanie Klein disagree about their origin, and I will here propose a reinterpretation of the phenomena by associating them with the psychological barriers that hinder money making.

There is a phantasy that goes by the name of "imago of the combined parent-figure," triggered by very primitive, archaic anxieties, and embodied by parental intercourse. In the phantasy, these two-in-one imply a tremendous threat to the child, both because of the power the figure represents and because it inscribes a state of permanent parental mutual gratification from which the child is excluded. You may argue that infants have no idea of what goes on behind the closed doors of their parents' bedroom. But this is happening at an unconscious level, at a very precocious stage of infantile sexual theories. The imago includes the extra ingredient that the mother incorporates the penis into her own body as an "evil" object, which contributes to the terrors but proves irrelevant to this analysis. Then we need to consider a mechanism called "introjection" which, roughly speaking, consists in absorbing external objects (and/or some of their characteristics) from real life into the psyche and creating fantasmatic "doubles" that do not actually depict these objects as a photograph would, for other mechanisms, including perception, cause distortions.

Let's assume that, in infancy, the four children introjected the parental couple constituted by Mrs. Vassilias and her husband as one object. The unconscious picture of this object may have had Mr. Vassilias's "frightening" aspects as its salient features. Consequently, the children were unconsciously afraid of the introjected object, but avoided defying their flesh-and-blood father, for in their psyche both the father and the introjection stood for one and the same person. Trying not to make this unnecessarily complicated, the evil aspects of partial or whole introjected objects belong more in archaic human fears than in any objective trait of the real object. But sometimes certain features of the real object attach themselves to the phantasy, and children grow up with an internal parental image whose mirror reflection they believe to be their real parents (the same would hold true for any other introjected object).

Defense mechanisms operate in a number of ways, as you may have read in *Living with Stress*. In this particular way, and in accordance with their personality traits, each of the children reacted differently to protect themselves of the threat they perceived as coming from their father when, if threat was indeed involved, it originated in the introjection of the imago. Notice that the elder daughter managed to step outside the economic circle that her father upheld through the extreme measure of pregnancy by someone she knew would be rejected by both parents, and then, having achieved independence through marriage, never accepted a second chance to go back to her previous life. The second daughter seemed to be in two minds about money, for she gave away her rightful inheritance while complaining that she could have put it to self-indulgent uses. The younger son expressed overt hostility against his father's way of life, fought it actively, and preferred to die rather than use his father's money to treat his illness. The elder son, who didn't seem to reject his father's views about money, did well *while* he stayed by his father's side, but then, when he expressed a wish to stand on his own two feet, destroyed everything he had the ability to build, as if to show his father that he had taught him well, but not well enough to free him from acting as a mere appendix to Dimitri. In other words, this son seemed to be pointing out that Dimitri had withheld from him the secret of lasting success.

In what way was the perceived threat associated to money? Mr. Vassilias's motto—not that he really had one, but it could be inferred from his speech—was best summed up in the phrase "money is the base of the family's stability." Not one day went by without his reminding his children that they owed their well-being to money and that, just in the same way as he had made a fortune from nothing, it was their duty to contribute to such fortune by marrying into money in the case of the girls and putting their education at the service of business expansion in the case of the boys. In their early childhood, these children entertained the phantasy that they had been fathered by a man called

Money. This is not a joke. The elder daughter posed the question about the father's name at the age of three. Having heard her mother refer to Mr. Vassilias as Mr. Money a number of times, and yet unaware of the existence of a last name, she asked, "Daddy, what's your name?" Her father found it funny, and asked her back, "Haven't you ever heard your mom calling my name?" "Yes," said the child, "but I've heard her call you Dimitri and also Mr. Money, so which is it?" Mr. Vassilias explained that the Mr. Money thing was a joke, told her about last names, and on the whole felt quite flattered at the nickname that Fatima circulated. Anyway, all this went far beyond the elder daughter's possibilities of comprehension, so the phantasy of having been begotten by an all-powerful, strong, mysterious Mr. Money stuck with her, and she later passed it on to her siblings. At a later age, the phantasy underwent a transformation. Mr. Money and Mr. Vassilias blended into one real person that the children loved but didn't like. At a conscious level, what they didn't like about him was that he measured people's qualities by their ability to relate to money. At an unconscious level, their motives differed.

The daughters' psyche seems to have persuaded them that if they married into money they would lose their own identity and become an appendix to their rich husbands or, that if they made money through their own efforts, they might turn into their father's feminine counterpart: ruthless women moving through life with a yardstick labeled "money."

The younger son clearly expressed his rejection of Mr. Vassilias's values. One may suspect that, besides other father-son issues at stake, his contact with the outside world (readings, leftist teachers, attendance to political meetings, etc.) inclined him to fight money as the source of all evils. The elder son's failure in keeping whatever money he made on his own sounded like a desperate scream that he had not reached the necessary degree of independence to let go, in very concrete terms, of his father's hand.

If you find a resemblance between you and any of the above unconscious choices, go to the corresponding questionnaire at the end of this part and work on the questions you will find there. You may discover that it is possible to replace "bad" total or partial introjected objects for "good" ones, and that this has great effects on your everyday life.

Having undergone individual processes of subject construction (a fact which highlights the uniqueness I so much insist on), the Karidis children managed their relation to money in accordance with their different perceptions of it. Although the starting point was shared by all four of them, they took individual decisions between adolescence and adulthood, and must be considered separately. With only one exception (that of the son who systematically built a fortune to lose it), the decision making process was conscious, although these young people never saw the unconscious mechanisms that urged them to live as they did.

As stated in before, the intriguing case lies with the son who attempted to follow into his father's footsteps. He reminds me of the finance manager at a very well known international company that earned millions thanks to his business ability. I knew that he was handsomely rewarded for this, but felt curious that he didn't consider starting his own company. "I can make money for others not for myself," he replied. I was struck by his clarity of mind no less than by the fact that he had no idea why things worked that way.

Remember that the young man in the story did exceedingly well managing his father's business and that I ascribed his later failures to an unspoken statement that he had not reached the necessary degree of independence from his father?

Once again, ambivalence enters the scene. Theo—let's call him so—felt quite comfortable in a business that his father had taught him well. On the other hand, at the unconscious level, it bothered him to have Mr. Karidis breathing down his neck all the time. We don't know whether or not this actually happened, but it was Theo's perception. Then, to him, it was true, and it diminished him in his own eyes.

Perhaps Mr. Karidis should have warned him that running his own business would not prove as simple as managing a well-oiled company that had been in the market for years. By way of justification, it could be argued that, having started from literally nothing to end up rolling in money, the father may have thought that Theo's project was infinitely easier. After all, he had had the best education that money could pay for, first hand experience of finance, and been lulled by money-related chitchat.

In fact, Theo showed that he was capable of making money. That he went bankrupt four times points to a failure in his idealized image and its connection to the introjected parental figure. His idealized image led him to believe that his economic know-how equaled his father's.

However, the introjected parental figure (a source of archaic anxieties) that he was unable to tell from his real father—as shown by Theo feeling Mr. Karidis "breathing down his neck"—contradicted his father's trust in him, shown through words of encouragement and money to get started. The prohibitory function of Theo's superego seemed to warn him against daring to rise to his father's levels of success. The four bankruptcies were the visible tips of a long, painful struggle to defeat the prohibition. Again, all this happened inside Theo's unconscious. Then perhaps we should surmise that what sounded like a scream for help, an unvoiced confession that he was not ready to stand on his own two feet, was in fact a rationalization that cut the bridges between Theo's unconscious motives to fail and his vision of such motives.

It's worth dwelling for a moment on the issue of rationalization, a concept that I'm introducing here for the first time. Although not acknowledged by a number of psychological/psychoanalytic theories, the concept proves useful to explain our interpretative mistakes when we try to understand why we do, say, or experience things whose logic escapes us. Rationalization is a defense mechanism that provides a "logical" explanation for facts that, if properly analyzed, would arouse/increase our anguish and/or lower our self-esteem. The use of "logical" between inverted commas is justified by the fact that the reasoning preceding the explanation is, in fact, a fallacy. Most of the authors for whom rationalization is a valid concept contend that it projects blame/responsibility outside the subject, thus freeing her from her own role in the problem. I would say that it's not always so. Sometimes, like in Theo's case, the subject remains implicated from his idealized image so, in a way, she's someone else.

When our economic goals fall to pieces, we tend to resort to this defense mechanism in order to avoid falling to pieces ourselves. Use the blank page/s at the end of this part to list down your rationalizations in the face of economic failure. Then try to discover the fallacy in them and seek a more truthful explanation through introspection.

2.5

Vinnie was the middle child in the Guarino family. The literature has much to say about "the middle child syndrome"; unfortunately, you will find that authors tend to contradict one another about what this implies. By way of example, while some say that the middle child usually lacks initiative, achieves no more than will keep him out of academic trouble at school, lacks the knack to make friends, and cannot make up her mind about practically anything, from what clothes to wear to what career to choose, others maintain that, depending on the role adopted by or assigned to the firstborn, the middle child will pick exactly the opposite behavior in an effort to differentiate herself. Thus, for example, if the elder sibling is quiet and friendly, the middle child will supposedly be boisterous and quarrelsome, and the other way about. To complicate things further, some say that the youngest sibling does not enter the equation, whereas others insist that the (internal) quarrel is with both, for in the middle child's view the parents ignore her to favor one of the other two. There are even those who include gender as part of the problem, warning us that the picture will vary depending on whether the two genders are involved.

No one in Vinnie's family even dreamed that the middle child syndrome existed, and I even doubt that they knew the meaning of "syndrome." Mr. Guarino and his wife Ida, both of Italian descent, had been raised to live by the same standards every Italian-American took pride in. They married young, had financial help from their parents to set up a restaurant that prospered amazingly fast and soon opened branches in several cities thanks to its patrons (the elite of the immigrant Italian community) and, when Ida got pregnant with Joey, their first, agreed that she should exchange the counter for the crib. Exactly one year after Joey's birth came Vinnie, and ten months later, Tony. Fathering three boys in a row fulfilled Mr. Guarino's best expectations. (For reasons that we will not discuss here, some men feel more virile when they have boys.) There were no money issues at the Guarinos'. They had enough and to spare, the father never used money or its equivalents as a control device, and he had a natural instinct not to give the wrong things at the wrong time, unlike one of his cousins, who insisted that his elementary school children wear gold watches just "to show them who we are." The "them" in question must have been the offspring of rich families attending the same school as his, only these families came from a different background and laughed at this pointless display of wealth behind the victims' backs, sometimes even to their face, depending on the occasion.

However, life at the Guarinos' wasn't exactly a bed

of roses. For no reason at all—at least for no detectable reason—not a day went by without a quarrel breaking out between husband and wife. Suddenly, the quiet atmosphere of their home was stormed by angry words, yelling, and Ida, a mess of sobs and tears, locked herself up in the master bedroom. The new day started as if nothing had happened, and ended exactly in the same havoc. Mr. Guarino was said to be an irascible, short-tempered man, a trait that he concealed when in company. Rumor had it that he took out his frustrations on his wife, and as the tiniest setback made him lose his cool, he had an inexhaustible source of frustrations to draw on.

Joey got used to this routine as one does to changes in the weather, but Vinnie became unspeakably frightened at the scenes and echoed his mother's sobs. From very early on, his father interrupted the volley of verbal abuse to his wife to address him as a "moron." As he grew up, his parents noticed that he was a bit slow on the uptake. It took him long to work through his school assignments, mostly because he didn't really understand what he was supposed to do. This earned him Joey's mockery, added to the fact that now "moron" became his first name, for his father didn't miss any opportunity to remind him of his shortcomings by calling him so. His mother never used the offending word, but she wondered in a loud voice why Vinnie wasn't as clever as his brothers, as smart as his only friend Petey, or as charming as the next door boy.

We don't know whether the scenes that Vinnie witnessed in infancy had some connection to his condition (the scenes went on forever, and at some point he stopped being consciously upset at them). What we do know is that he accepted parental and brotherly abuse as a matter of course. Perhaps it should be said that Tony had no part in this. To him, Vinnie was something like a piece of furniture. You don't talk to a piece of furniture.

When Vinnie graduated from secondary school, both his teachers and his friend Petey encouraged him to pursue further studies. They told him it would demand focusing and effort, but that he would get all the help he needed. For once, Vinnie came out of his apathy and spoke of college prospects at home. Mr. Guarino wouldn't hear of it. "What's the point?" he grunted. "You barely made it through school. I'll get you something to do at the restaurant. That's your best bet, considering." Vinnie made a weak attempt at keeping the conversation going. For once in his life, he felt he had to stand up to his father. "Shut up, you moron!" shouted his father, and engaged in a row with Ida, accusing her of putting ideas into Vinnie's head. Poor Ida didn't have an inkling of what he was talking about!

So Joey and Tony went to college, in due time managed the restaurants, and Vinnie remained an underpaid jack of all trades. He never complained, didn't seem interested in making money and, when he got married to a girl of humble origin who wanted more ("It's your right, Vinnie; for God's sakes, think of our children!") he replied once and again that morons can love and be loved and raise families but cannot make money.

If you have read *Living with Stress*, you may remember how we determine who we are, and that certain personality types construct an idealized image (a false self). A very complex process, the construction of the self includes, among many other things, the ways in which we see ourselves reflected in meaningful others, conveyed by their attitude to us *and by the names they call us*. Years of the word "moron" used as a synonym for Vinnie finally caused him to identify his self with this term. In the book mentioned, I told you that we constantly try to confirm or disconfirm our perceptions by contrasting them with what we know and with facts. In his thirties, Vinnie "knew" what his father taught him through endless repetition, came across a couple of newspaper articles about the middle child's personality and never doubted their content (the value of truth ascribed to the printed word, especially the press, is indeed shocking). In addition, his intellectual difficulty to keep up with his peer group confirmed what he "knew" from the first two sources. The first book of this series also warned you that these beliefs are dangerous insofar as they can furnish you with a completely mistaken idea of who you are and of what external facts mean. However, this is what happened to Vinnie, and the reason why he couldn't make money was grounded on obedience to an internalized parental mandate. Supposing we add up the repeated epithet and his mother's regrets about his not being clever, smart, or charming, plus his father's refusal to send him to college plus his decision that Vinnie should not be entrusted with managerial decisions because he would sink the business, we come up with a very strong mandate: *You shall not make money*. In his heart of hearts, Vinnie obeyed this mandate all his life. And the saddest thing is that he thought that his own nature/personality/weakness of character prevented him from getting out of the swamp of mediocrity in which he lived.

You may be tricked into believing that, in this story, it would seem as if the middle-child syndrome played a significant part in Vinnie's acceptance of a dull (and moneyless) future. Because of the widespread belief that middle children bear the brunt of either ill treatment or indifference in the family, one could easily make a mistaken association between his status and his failure. However, this belief is belied by a large number of cases, perhaps not taken into account by the literature, in which middle children are compensated, generally during or after adolescence, for real or imaginary injuries. This may result from the parents feeling guilty about not having given this child the whole of their time and attention as they did with the firstborn and from further neglect when the third baby arrived. The mechanism of overcompensation (excessive leniency, permissiveness, better clothes and larger allowances) is more frequently found than that of mere compensation. In practice, a middle child who never got either kind of compensation and one who did seem to end up with problems. The former tends to have low self-esteem, which may be translated into utter meekness or unusual violence, depending on the surrounding circumstances, while the latter shows inflated levels of self-esteem leading to life-risk situations, for these children identify with the superhero of your choice.

My point is that Vinnie's fate wouldn't have been different in terms of moneymaking had he been later compensated for his random birth order. What turned him into a failure was a matter of language.

The abstract of an article entitled *Signification and the Unconscious,* by Grant Gillet, vividly describes the connection between language and the unconscious: "[. . .] The mental content of the subject is essentially tied to the external world both causally and linguistically. The means of tying the two together arise in the context of human interactions and are charged with personal and emotive content. [. . .] much of its meaning and significance to a subject [derive from] the interpersonal medium through which it has been inscribed on that subject. [. . .]"

Let me try to reduce the level of abstraction of this enlightening paper and see if I can establish a modest connection between the central idea above and the role that language played in Vinnie's development toward nothingness.

Denotative aspects of language, called "grade 0" in Spanish, convey only such meanings as have been agreed upon by the speech community. Denotation amounts to the code function of language and, precisely because the code is at work, it's practically impossible for different receivers to introduce meanings beyond the convention and the context in which the utterances are made. In other words, when at dinnertime someone says "The food is on the table," every receiver present will share exactly the same representations. They know the isolated denotative meanings of all the words said, and in what way each of these words relates to the others in the chain. This kind of language is mostly used for factual communication, and fulfills its purpose successfully. The weight of my example and similar utterances lies in a correct syntactic arrangement not on either the speaker or the receiver.

On the other hand, the connotative function of language points to extended/suggested/associated meanings that may or may not include the primary code meaning. In this mode, the sender and the receiver matter. Outside the code function, words that come from a parent/sibling/spouse/friend, just to offer a few examples, are emotionally charged and perceived. The inscription of such words, particularly when repetition is the rule, resembles branding by fire.*

Using the structure of a question, Mrs. Guarino complained about Vinnie's lack of intellectual and social skills. She never addressed him directly, but the boy was present, and the context guaranteed that he understood who was the intended receiver of the "I wonder" series. I don't agree that the mother tongue can be roughly equated to the mother's tongue. The mother's tongue (your mother's; the tongue of a flesh-and-blood mother speaking to or about a flesh-and-blood child) can easily do you or undo you. Your perception assumes that you are what and who she says you are. No doubt you can reverse this notion as is explained in *Living with Stress*. Many people never learn of the possibility.

---

* Most people don't seem aware that, in a way, language constructs reality. If you're offered a delicious dish that tastes of chicken and are then told you've eaten snake, you'll probably throw up on the spot. What changed? Just a word that brings up feelings of repugnance. That they then tell you it was a practical joke will not change your frame of mind. In the past, as proved by anthropological studies, shamans induced even death through verbal suggestion techniques.

Perhaps Mr. Guarino thought that "moron" connoted nothing special, although its denotative meaning is negative enough. One might even give him the benefit of the doubt and suppose that, for him, the word had the semantic value of an interjection. Again, look at the context and the father-son relationship. In his infancy, Vinnie had no idea what the wretched word meant, but he perceived the tone of voice, the anger, and the fact that neither of his brothers was "blessed" with this epithet. When he learned the dictionary meanings (stupid, idiot, imbecile, fool) or at least one of them, he incorporated associated connotations such as "good for nothing," "pain in the ass," and "mentally retarded." Here the connotations acted as extensions of the denotation. Moreover, with his brothers' joining in, his father treated him as if he were less than regularly human, and his mother didn't object. Silence gives consent. The mandate that Vinnie's superego imposed on him summed up the linguistic and situational interactions to which he had been subjected.

If you feel that you have something in common with Vinnie, whether or not you are a middle child, go to the blank pages at the end of this part and answer the questions about your case. Disengaging from inner mandates that you cannot recognize as such will help you begin to trust in your own judgement without fearing the anger of the superego, the component of the psychic apparatus that at times may constitute a life saver and at other times may censor your legitimate wishes to the point of paralysis.

2.6

One last story to close the sample section. Ernest Meersch, a sensible furrier who invested wisely and amassed a small fortune with the help of his wife Ann, who was a great administrator and a mother of four sons, raised their children in a way that contradicted the rules that he himself conformed to.

These children lived a privileged childhood, attended the best schools, and owned the most expensive toys the market offered. Ann saw to it that they learned to share with less fortunate friends, always subtly remarking that they were enjoying the advantages of having a moneyed father. The subliminal message was that in due time they were expected to do the same by their own families.

All four were exceptional students and gained admission at prestigious universities. Three became lawyers and one a physician. The minute they graduated, Ernest set them up in private practice and referred his wide circle of friends and acquaintances to his brilliant sons, who soon found suitable brides and brought new babies into the family. It goes without saying that Ernest's wedding present to each of his sons consisted of a comfortable, fully furnished and equipped house or apartment of their choice.

Having plenty of free time now that the children were gone, Ann made a point of dropping by at least once a week. Her keen eye noticed that her daughters-in-law didn't look happy and changed the subject when she brought up their husbands' busy schedules. With remarkable tact she managed to draw the girls out and make them feel at ease to talk about what troubled them. Thus she found out that her sons were not doing well for the simple reason that they neglected their commitments to their clients. She couldn't believe her ears, but what shocked her off her feet was to learn, from her husband's own lips, that he knew about it and that he also stopped by his sons' weekly to ask them how much they needed without a word of reproach.

A serious argument ensued. Ann firmly warned her husband that he must stop treating their sons as if they were still children. Ernest waved the matter away. "We spoiled them from day one. They need time to get used to the idea that they are grown-up men. You surely don't expect me to let them starve in the meantime, do you?"

"Buying Isaac a timeshare is letting him starve?" exploded Ann. "Can't you find the courage to tell them that you'll pay for their basic needs for one more month, and that's it? Well, if you can't, I will. They've watched you work all your life. You could've retired years ago, but you're still working. What's wrong with these kids?"

Good question. A question that contained the answer. Keyword: kids. The Meersch brothers had developed their intellect, but not grown emotionally. They loved money, but lacked the psychic tools to take their lives in their hands and stop feeling like kids under dad's protective wings. Both parents had fostered some kind of blissful unreality in which these sons dwelt. They were not prepared to make money even when they had they the tools because, in their unconscious mind, they had not crossed the bridge that would have enabled them to leave childhood and adolescence behind (i.e., cast aside their internal father) in order to constitute themselves as fathers. The imbalance between intellectual and emotional growth is more usual than many people imagine, and a significant factor in the impossibility of making money for, after all, making money belongs in the realm of adulthood. Sometimes unconscious refusal to give up emotional dependence on a parent/parents assumes a variety of disguises, but one needs to recognize them as such and get rid of them before they turn into a second skin.

Excessive parental pampering in childhood and adolescence results in handicapped adults. I have often heard, "The world the child will have to contend with is cruel enough. Why not pamper her now to make up in advance for the harshness she will come up against?" I regret to say that parents who support the idea that pampering will serve as a "cushion" to protect and brace up their offspring when they need to confront life are wrong. What we usually call "spoilt children" have indeed been spoiled in the original meaning of the word: ruin/prevent something from being successful or satisfactory. The "something" are the children, who have been deprived of the opportunity to grow up. Not having learned to wait for and earn the things they desire, flooded to the point of metaphorically drowning in the sea of generic concrete and abstract objects that their parents lavish on them, these spoon-fed children find themselves at a clear disadvantage when they need to move ahead by themselves. While their only resources seem to be tantrums, hysterical behavior, or running to a surrogate parent (a boss, for example) for help, their competitors, suitably trained in struggling for their goals, will always have the upper hand. This is especially true in the economic area, where you don't get to succeed by simply flashing a smile at the sources of money.

Not much can be added about the Meersch brothers. Alfred Adler, an Austrian physician and psychologist who collaborated with Freud until they parted ways because of irreconcilable theoretical differences, posed that violent criminals had experienced parental pampering in childhood. Supposedly, when these children grew up and were expected to work for what they wanted, they just helped themselves to it even if this implied taking human lives in the process. Modern criminology maintains, on statistical grounds, that far from having been pampered children, violent criminals were victims of neglect, abuse, or both during childhood.

The main trouble with the Meersch brothers was that their emotional growth became impaired by their parents' (especially their father's) misconception of parental love. When you're raising a child, "no" and other negative phrases may pierce your heart, but prove most effective to build a strong subject that will learn to defeat obstacles, to persist in her goals, and to crave for adulthood so that she can pursue her desires.

Pampered children tend to develop into frustrated creatures that look like adults but indulge in infantile fantasies, especially those that involve magic thought; i.e., that it's enough to wish for something to make it happen. Well, it certainly isn't enough to wish for money to find it in your pockets. Some gamblers seem to fall into this category, although a thorough study of gambling habits would reveal other, really disturbing basic aspects of personality.

Alternately, pampered children whose parents never leave them to their own devices (the case under discussion) consider themselves luckier than people who struggle for a living. Like the ones I described earlier, they also live in a fantasy world, but it's a different kind of fantasy, for they lack nothing, and expect to come into money at their parents' demise. This makes them careless and irresponsible in economic matters, since Dad will always be there (part of the fantasy; Dad can well have invested all his assets with Lehman Brothers, for example) to clean up the mess.

For the last twenty years or so, we have heard of the phenomenon of prolonged adolescence. This is no place to expand on the subject, but I guess you know exactly how it works. The Meersch brothers seem to fit the requirements, except that many members of this group go through the motions of adult life, including making money, but shun responsibility for their social, family, and economic roles in society.

If you suspect that your impossibility to make money is due to prolonged adolescence, answer the questions on the blank page/s at the end of this part.

If you think that you have something else in common with the Meersch brothers, go to the blank pages at the end of this part and go over the introspection exercises you will find there. Your love bond with your parent/s will remain as strong as ever from the right, adult, responsible place in the family structure.

2.7

Sometimes being a parent, whether rich, average-income, or poor, seems to imply some kind of tacit guilt related to what you give your children. Roughly speaking, parents could be divided into two categories: those who think "what was good/enough for me should be good for my children" and those who are convinced that "I had to make do with very little, and am ready to work my fingers to the bones so that my children don't have to experience the deprivations that I suffered." Even if it's not actually necessary for the second group to flay their fingers (they may be already well off), these are the ones on whom guilt preys.

Sons and daughters may not come up to your expectations of them in terms of, say, academic achievement, but during childhood they've had ample time to study *you*, and they get straight A's in the subject How to Press my Mother's/Father's Guilt Buttons.

You may not be aware of this, but every time you failed to fulfill a promise such as attending a school concert in which your child performed, or take her to a game because you were held up at the office (recall examples from your own life), your child's disappointment triggered guilty feelings in you. Although not every child reacts in the same way—some just give you a reproachful look, others vent their frustration through language, and still others play indifferent, as if they didn't care—the effect on you is the same. You begin to feel in debt, and are probably prone to pay with interest at the wrong time, which is when they make an unreasonable demand in later life. Because of the guilt mechanism, the more you have pampered your children the more you will give in to their extortive practices. There are two main reasons why sons and daughters grow into "professional" blackmailers. One is the record they consciously or unconsciously keep of the times you let them down, regardless of whether you had good reasons to do so and/or it didn't depend on you. The other is that you yourself took on the appearance of an all-powerful parent. When both aspects blend in your offspring's psyche, the string of unreasonable requests begins. Their whole future will be ruined (such is one of the many arguments you hear) unless you pay for a ridiculously expensive—and useless—course taught at the other end of the world. They must take a year off to travel around (at your expense) so as to expand their knowledge of other countries and cultures. What will their friends and, most importantly, their friends' parents think if *your* children drive an inexpensive car? And so forth.

Don't be deluded into thinking that the issue is money. Certainly, money plays a major role in these requests. Still, in all likelihood, the true, not always unconscious issue is retribution for the unfairness you supposedly put them through in the past.

If you have pampered your children without restraint, there's very little you can do to put things into perspective. Of course you can refuse to oblige, supposing you're ready to pay the price. Let me tell you that the suffering on your part will be much more expensive than complying with this sort of request. The offended youth/adult will estrange herself from you, not return your calls, and generally act "dead." What might help would be to have a heart-to-heart conversation with her, try to make her understand what you did wrong (the pampering) and why it was wrong, and suggest turning over a new leaf, changing your relationship to one in which responsibility and common sense prevails on both parts.

The best solution is to avoid excessive pampering from the very beginning, which means that you need to work on your guilt issues as you go along. Introspection isn't a mechanical tool that you turn on when things look difficult to be discarded until the next problem appears. It's a daily activity, as essential as breathing. Just in case your guilty feelings overwhelm you, let me tell you one last story.

The Carrs were an extremely rich family living in accordance with their economic and social status. Their children partook of this lifestyle, but were not pampered in any way. However, they shared their school life with others whose parents behaved differently. This had an effect on the elder son who, on turning twenty-one asked, as if it were the most natural thing in the world, to spend an idle year in Paris "to improve his French in everyday situations." Mr. Carr told him straightaway that being rich involved serious social responsibility to the less fortunate. Therefore, said Mr. Carr, "you will do your duty as our family has always done. When and if you make money by yourself, you're welcome to put it to whatever use you like. In the meantime, remember it's family money you're planning to squander. This is appropriation of resources that are not yet yours, and I will not allow it. However, even though I thoroughly disapprove of the idea, you can find your way to Paris and seek sustenance by finding a job." Needless to say, young Carr promptly abandoned his project.

What I'd like you to see, apprehend, and adopt as second nature, is that perhaps you *are* guilty of a number of things, but that yielding to blackmail isn't the way to make amends. You cannot make guilt go away by pouring money into your children's hands. You need to clear up what's wrong with *you* and then help them see where they're mistaken, leaving blame out of the picture.

You are now ready to enter the realm of fear, one of the most paralyzing hindrances to moneymaking.

Questionnaires

THE "KEVIN" TYPE

1. As a child, did you miss your parents' presence?
2. As a child/teenager, did you try to draw their attention by unconsciously misbehaving/making friends with the wrong people/getting into dangerous situations that required their intervention?
3. If so, how did they respond?
4. If not, how did you feel about their not responding?
5. As a young adult, did you ever look back on your childhood and adolescence and try to find reasons for what you perceived as your parents' indifference?
6. Did you ever speak to them about how their attitude made you feel? If you did, what did they say? If you didn't, explain why not.
7. Can you honestly say that you do not/did not love your parents? Write down the facts that support your answer.
8. To what extent do you blame your parents for your present circumstances?
9. Do you believe you could have made independent decisions about your relation to money once you had become more experienced in the ways of the world? Please elaborate on this.
10. Make a list of the positive and negative messages you perceived from your parents' behavior to you.

POSITIVE

NEGATIVE

Now try to reinterpret your history. Write down how you could move on after revisiting the past.

THE "STELLA" TYPE

1. When your parents quarreled about money, did they notice the effect this had on you? If so, did either of them try to comfort you?
2. Did you ever perceive that your mother might have been right?
3. If you didn't, can you rethink now the extent to which some of the things she demanded were fair? Please elaborate on this.
4. Did your father ever talk to you about money? What did he say?
5. As a teenager, did you ever wonder about your father's attitude to money? Did you try to take up the matter with him?
6. As a young adult, did it occur to you that you were repeating your father's attitude to money? If so, how did you explain this to yourself?
7. How do you rationalize your not doing anything to earn more in order to achieve goals that demand money?
8. If you can now realize that a) you are *not* your father and, b) your father would be proud of you if you surpassed his financial achievements, please elaborate on how you could make the most of your new knowledge.

THE "KARIDIS ELDER DAUGHTER" TYPE

1. You married beneath you in economic terms. Did you ever consider the pros and cons of your decision? Please list them down.
2. Did you expect your husband to rise to your father's economic level? Explain what prompted you to do so/ not to do so.

THE "KARIDIS ELDER AND YOUNGER DAUGHTER" TYPE

3. Did you ever feel relieved that you no longer depended on your father? If so, why?
4. You probably didn't feel comfortable around your father as from early adolescence. Explain what he did/ said as you perceived it that made you uneasy.
5. How did you view your mother's role in the couple? Please elaborate on this.
6. What bothered you about your father's wealth?

THE "KARIDIS YOUNGER DAUGHTER" TYPE

7. In what way do you think that rejecting men in general might rid you of your father? Did it work?
8. Do you regret your choice? If so, write down how you could have the best of both worlds without losing independence.

THE "KARIDIS YOUNGER SON" TYPE

1. Consider that by turning down your father you unconsciously believed that all the evils of Capitalism would go away. Has your outlook changed? If so, explain why.

2. Did it ever occur to you that economic inequality (or, at least a part of it) can be changed through a wise use of money? Please write down how the money you rejected could have aided your goals.

THE "KARIDIS YOUNGER AND ELDER SON" TYPE

3. Did you ever feel relieved that you no longer depended on your father? If so, why?

4. You probably didn't feel comfortable around your father as from early adolescence. Explain what he did/ said as you perceived it that made you uneasy.

5. How did you view your mother's role in the couple? Please elaborate on this.

6. What bothered you about your father's wealth?

THE "KARIDIS ELDER SON" TYPE

7. What do you think you could have learned from the experience of losing your first fortune?

8. What role do you think your introjected parent-figure played in your economic failure/s?

9. Were you unconsciously competing with your father and fearing imaginary punishment if you won? Or were you trying to send him an SOS message because you didn't feel mature enough to stand in his shoes? Consider this carefully before answering.

MY RAZIONALIZATIONS IN THE FACE OF ECONOMIC FAILURE AND THE FALLACY BEHIND EACH OF THEM

THE "VINNIE" TYPE

1. Do you recall your parents using disparaging language to/about you when you were a child? List down what you remember.
2. How did you feel when this happened?
3. At what point in your life did you become convinced that you deserved such epithets?
4. When you contrasted the way you were treated at home with external, objective reality, what made you feel that the truth lay in what you experienced at home?
5. Can you identify negative parental mandates that affected your relation to money? Please list them down.
6. Are you ready to establish a separation between these mandates and your potential? Write down what you think you are good at that might bring you money.
7. How does disparaging language affect you today? Please elaborate on this.

THE "MEERSCH BROTHERS" TYPE

a) PROLONGED ADOLESCENCE

1. Do you think that life is long enough for you to take your time and indulge in today's pleasures before formally entering the adult world? If so, how did you come by this idea?

2. As an adult, does it not bother you to be economically dependent on a parent? What do you think lies at the bottom of your dependence?

3. If you have a family of your own, what do you think your spouse feels about your attitude to life?

4. Have you and your spouse discussed your happy-go-lucky view of responsibility? What arguments were expressed by each of you?

5. Do you believe you have the right to keep others on tenterhooks about your economy? Please elaborate on this.

b) OTHER CHARACTERISTICS

6. How did your father's behavior in life and his behavior to you differ?

7. Did your father speak to you about responsibility or did he just hope that you would learn from watching him?

8. In your present circumstances, how do you view your upbringing?

DEEPER INTROSPECTION

1. Write down how you truly feel you will move on in life without your father's help.
2. Make a list of the tools you lack to achieve full economic independence. Lay out a plan to acquire these tools. **Avoid rationalizing about this.**

3

3.1

The faces of fear

That fear of making money is one of the reasons for some people's failure at it might sound at best ridiculous and at worst delusional. However, it ranks high on the list of obstacles to a satisfactory approach to economic success. You don't need to be told about the externalization of fear, for you must be/must have been afraid of something for short or long spans. Perhaps if we take a look at the neurobiological and psychological factors that determine fear it will be easier for you to see that not every fear is apparent. In other words, sometimes you simply don't consciously know that you're afraid.

Fear, one of the most primitive human emotions, is easily recognizable through physical symptoms such as difficulty breathing, sweaty hands, alterations in the cardiac rhythm, stomach cramps, and a feeling of paralysis. Another important thing to bear in mind is that fear is triggered by a given object, be it a fire arm or a perception of some impending threat. Unlike stress, fear subsides once the object is removed and comes back when the object reappears unless you inquire into the reasons why that particular object makes you afraid. I would remark that there's nothing frightening in the objects themselves but that your unconscious associations invest them with their fearsome characteristics. If you manage to make these associations conscious, you will get rid of your fears. Exception made of some fears that we seem to harbor in our collective unconscious (fear of snakes, for instance) there isn't a catalog of "things to be afraid of." Our fears follow the patterns of our uniqueness.

Last but not least, although most of the reactions that warn us that we are in the clutches of fear come from the body, fear itself begins and ends in the brain, more specifically in the hypothalamus, an evolutionary relic of our development into humans whose role and importance remained unknown until relatively recent times (the first discovery of one of its many functions dates back to the late 19th century).

The point is that you don't include money on your list of feared objects or life events. Thus, when the possibility of making money comes into the picture, two things may happen: the physical signals appear and you attribute them to some other object or fact, or your psyche intervenes by rationalizing your rejection/creating defense mechanisms to justify your withdrawal.

What could make you afraid of making money? There are as many answers as people who experience this particular phenomenon. Let's name a few, and if you feel that a different kind of fear has been hindering you from taking the challenges that need overcoming, use the blank page/s at the end of this chapter to describe your case in detail.

To begin with, money entails responsibility. By responsibility I mean not only a rational use of resources, but also decisions that affect others and changes in your lifestyle that perhaps you're not ready to cope with.

3.2

My father-in-law was a skilled factory worker who, because of his intelligence, natural curiosity to always learn more by watching and analyzing managerial decisions, self-teaching through books about his special tasks, and proven loyalty to the company, was eventually promoted to an executive position in his area of expertise. He was elated and content that this was his roof. Of course his economic status improved considerably. Now he could afford a better house, buy a car (his first), and take the family on vacations to great beauty spots in Argentina, his country.

My mother-in-law insisted on his going for more. She would serve him breakfast, lunch and dinner with an additional, verbal side dish: "You can partner up with someone else and start your own company." Her husband tried to convince her that they were just fine now. He had a nine to seven job, time to spend with the family, and money to spare. What he didn't say, and probably didn't consciously realize, was that someone else had to worry so that his handsome salary was punctually paid, and that the responsibility of keeping the factory going fell on someone else as well. The conscious message from his brain was that he didn't care for more than he had achieved.

However, like the proverbial drop of water, a wife's tongue can bore through a rock, so eventually my father-in-law started to contemplate the possibility of becoming an entrepreneur, on equal terms with the so far unreachable (in terms of money) owner of the factory he worked for. He talked to a couple of mechanical engineers who might be interested in contributing capital and know-how, laid out the plans for the new company, and asked for an interview with Dr. Brukmann, the almighty head of the board of directors.

The owner-to-be felt that giving notice in the usual way (a telegram) implied disrespect to a man who had been fair and generous to him, so he wanted to tell him in person that he was leaving. Dr. Brukmann listened attentively, and said, "I'm not happy to lose you. Still, you have the talent and the initiative to succeed. I wish you the very best of luck, and hope to become your first client." (My father-in-law was planning on manufacturing spare parts that this and other factories outsourced.)

The preparatory work leading to the opening day kept my father-in-law away from home days, nights, and weekends. His wife's temper soured a bit, but she checked herself every time reproach came to her lips thinking that things would go back to normal afterward.

Finally, the new company started business. In a way, there were changes, but not the ones my mother-in-law anticipated. Her husband still spent "too long" at the job, and when he came home he inadvertently became deaf to conversation. Now he had deep frown lines that looked like a birthmark. Worst of all, the money he brought home was sometimes less than the salary he used to earn. This company more or less kept its head above water for five years, until my father-in-law sold his shares to his partners, who quickly turned it into something else. He went back to Dr. Brukmann asking for his old job if possible, or for whatever job available. Dr. Brukmann refrained from asking what had gone wrong and reinstated him in the Maintenance Department. Interestingly, my mother-in-law felt relieved at the step backward, and that was the end of the adventure.

3.3

But, indeed, what had happened? My parents-in-law honestly believed that he had not risen to the occasion, that he didn't have the makings of a true entrepreneur, that he had overestimated or underestimated the odds; in one word, that he hadn't been born to make money.

This was their rationalization. They never knew that they both were afraid. Let's see what fears operated in each of them.

My father-in-law felt unspeakably uneasy when he had to hold meetings with clients. Since his partners kept part-time professional jobs until the company "really took off," he couldn't delegate these meetings to them. Because he didn't have a degree, he was afraid of talking to educated men like Dr. Brukmann (only Dr. Brukmann was a familiar character) and being rejected or laughed at behind his back because of his curt language. Thus he either kept postponing meetings until the clients got impatient and commissioned the work to some other company, or became so inarticulate that the client entertained serious doubts about his capacity to deliver.

Like every other owner of a small company, he dealt

with his workers directly. He had done so too during his previous managerial experience, but the difference lay in the fact that in those times he had the board's support; in the workers' imagination (and probably in his own as well), he was simply the one who conveyed decisions made by others. In his own business, he found it difficult to acknowledge the hierarchical differences that separated him from his workers. He somehow expected to be contradicted, disobeyed, or challenged by former equals. In other words, he never internalized his new status.

Quite often clients delayed payments. Every time the end of a fortnight drew near, it worried him sick that the company would be short of money to pay wages. Since the policy was "wages and overheads first, and distribution of surplus among partners last," more than once did he and his partners forego their share to meet their obligations. However, the other two partners had the extra income from their part-time jobs, whereas my father-in-law depended solely on the business proceeds. What if things got really thick? A bank loan would have been the obvious answer. This was in fact suggested over and over again by his partners. Still, my father-in-law reasoned that they might have just as much trouble paying the bank as they had paying wages, the difference being that if they got in arrears with the bank they might well lose the collateral (the company).

His partners encouraged him to take golfing lessons and join a golf club. "A lot of good business comes from a couple of hours on the golf links," they said. And they practiced what they preached, but as they were not the hands-on experts, my father-in-law's presence would have been crucial to clinch a number of deals. After putting up some resistance, he dutifully engaged a coach and began playing golf. But after the golfing came the social engagements: drinks, card games, outings with wives/girl-friends. This is where he sensed he would feel completely out of his depth through lack of trust in his social skills. Leaving the golf course immediately after the game was over earned him a reputation of "a pretentious upstart," exactly the opposite of what he really was.

Then, my father-in-law was afraid of rebuff, of failure to show authority when he had to, of not meeting his financial obligations, of getting indebted, and of showing his inner feeling of inferiority among other things. Only he didn't know fear lurked behind the mask of generalized discomfort and preoccupation, and would never have admitted the truth, for none of the physical symptoms mentioned before were apparent, and he attributed the only physical signal—inarticulate speech—to his poor education.

Now, what was my mother-in-law afraid of? While pestering her husband with demands for more money and a change in social status, she viewed herself as some rich lady in a soap opera, wearing the latest fashion, entertaining my father-in-law's new acquaintances, attending fundraisers and dinner parties, ordering about the hired help, and enjoying life in grand style, more or less the way Tevye pictured his Golde in *Fiddler on the Roof.*

When my father-in-law started anew in life, she was unable to suitably accompany the changes (periods when money flowed in, periods when money was the same or less as before). She was the last daughter of an aristocratic but seriously impoverished family, so by the time she should have been taking singing and piano lessons under the vigilant eye of a French governess, for so were the customs of the times in Argentina, she was sent to an Arts and Crafts school so that she could make a living as a seamstress. Despite her upper class origins, my mother-in-law was, in practical terms, working class.

She longed to enjoy what she had missed from childhood on. When her husband was promoted at the factory, the economic condition of the family took a turn for the better, but the changes didn't involve social occasions. On the other hand, and for different reasons, the couple shied away from the socializing aspects required by money-making policies. The fact is that, confronted with the opportunity to help out her husband by joining him, as did other wives, in the after-golf club activities, dinners, etc. my mother-in-law realized that, even though she could spend money on her appearance, she had no idea about the "latest fashion" in a circle unknown to her, loathed having to ask for advice, since that would evidence her being an outsider, and intuited that she would play a poor role in the small talk in which the "ladies" surely engaged.

My mother-in-law was afraid of spoiling her husband's image through her inadequacy (she was obviously unaware of his own mistrust of himself), of being criticized by the other women, of not being accepted as an equal, and of reliving the humiliations that she had undergone as a seamstress not because of her job but because of her last aristocratic name, a name that caused much mirth and sniggering among her co-workers. In short, her drive to encourage her husband worked positively while the whole thing was a dream about to come true, but her shortcomings, unrecognized for what they were—fear, pure and simple—played a significant part in the failure of the project.

3.4

The type of personality that experiences fear and guilt more frequently than is normal may do everything within her power to succeed and, at the very last minute or shortly after success has been achieved, make a "fatal mistake" that will bring the laborious construction down with a resounding bang. Alternately, she may reach the same outcome (failure) through the sort of illness that requires peace, quiet, rest and, above all, a long spell free of worries. Heart attacks, strokes, car accidents, and multiple fracture falls are examples of this.

Myriam Endicott lost her mother in her early childhood. Mrs. Endicott hadn't been a patient woman, and one afternoon, after failing to get four-year old Myriam to drink her milk, she had stormed out of the house for some fresh air because she sensed that if the child put aside her cup once more she might slap her hard for lack of further persuasive arguments. She was so immersed in her anger and frustration that she practically threw herself in front of a bus and died instantly.

Of course no one blamed the child. However, the magic thought typical of the age associated the fact that she had strongly opposed her mother (and hated her for her insistence) with Mrs. Endicott's subsequent death. With the passing of time, Myriam's memories of the moment became blurred, all the more so because her father was extra careful to keep the mother alive as a "protective angel" now residing in some star but refrained from speaking about what had happened immediately before the mournful episode.

While in high school, Myriam conceived of a dream. The small town she lived in was historically important in terms of the American Revolution. One decisive battle had been fought nearby, and historians and archeologists from the big city came from time to time seeking relics and memorabilia in order to support their theoretical works. But the town had only one zero-star hotel, so it occurred to Myriam that if she could buy it and refurbish it, or have a new, comfortable one built, followed by a nationwide marketing campaign extolling the natural beauty and historical meaning of the place, tourists would swarm in to her own advantage and that of the town.

Throughout her childhood, adolescence, and early youth, Myriam was never able to overcome disturbing feelings that gripped her whenever someone close to her underwent some mishap. She was smart enough to identify these feelings as guilt, though it puzzled her that she felt guilty for things in which she had had no part.

Eventually, she obtained a Master in Business Administration with a Major in Hotel Management and returned to her hometown to try to get the Town Hall and small business owners interested in the project. The major promised to help with the marketing campaign if she obtained the necessary capital to put up the hotel, while the small businessmen pooled in their resources, formed a company presided by Myriam, and negotiated a loan with the local bank.

Under her father's guidance—for Mr. Endicott happened to be a respected contractor in the area before retiring—Myriam and her crew walked every step of the way until the hotel was ready to open its doors. There were setbacks, quarrels among the partners, and all the difficulties that have to be taken in stride when a business depends on so many people. Whenever an argument broke out, Myriam felt it was her fault, either because she had spoken the wrong words or because she had abstained from speaking.

Her father made her understand that she couldn't take responsibility for what others did and said, and pointed out that she needed to stick to her role, which for the moment was mainly to deal with suppliers; in fact, she would bear *all* of the responsibility only after the hotel was functioning.

The Board had organized a well thought-out program of events for the opening, set for a Friday evening and including the staging of a mocked parley between the American and the British general who had led the troops to victory and defeat respectively on the historic field.

A dress rehearsal would take place a few hours before the opening. Two reputed actors had agreed to play the generals. Everyone involved in the project was anxiously waiting for them and getting exceedingly anxious that, at that rate, the men would barely make it for the actual ceremony. At some point, they suspected that they had been played. In an effort to calm them down, Myriam ran to her office to show them her letter of invitation and their note of acceptance. She blindly thrust both into the hands of one of the partners, and was perplexed at the look he gave her. Mr. Greyson passed the letters around. An angry whisper of disbelief rose to a volley of curses. Mr. Greyson picked up the papers from the shaking hands of the last reader and asked in a cold, spiteful voice, "Could our General Manager please indicate where she wrote the date of the event? In a letter to the Electricity Company, perhaps?" Myriam couldn't believe her eyes as she scanned her letter of invitation. It contained the purpose, the request, the location . . . but not the date. Naturally, after having accepted, the two busy actors must have expected a second letter that never arrived because she thought she had given them all the particulars in the only one she wrote. My guess is that they forgot about the matter altogether or, that if it crossed their minds, they believed that the project had fallen through for some reason.

It goes without saying that the Board unanimously voted to oust Myriam. On this occasion she was indeed "guilty as charged." Her thundering failure at her most cherished dream sent her back to various anonymous, unpromising jobs, without ever again trying to undertake serious business.

3.5

What was Myriam afraid of? The traumatic experience of her mother's death established an unconscious pattern of guilt. In our culture, the only cure for guilt, real or imaginary, is punishment. Myriam felt that she had to be punished while she feared the moment when punishment would catch up with her. The sense of guilt that haunts many people is usually rooted in some forgotten (repressed) early incident. Guilt and fear of/desire for punishment tend to be very hard to disentangle. Those who make this kind of mistake or give themselves a serious illness are just creating the conditions for the punishment they feel they deserve. In short, the "great crime" they believe to have committed makes them unworthy of success, especially of economic success, for how could they enjoy the luxuries provided by wealth when their psyche (the superego, in these cases) torments them for having escaped retribution? Think on it.

3.6

The last case I'd like to present is fear of being dispossessed. People who tend to distrust their own shadow will not recognize what's going on in their psyche. They usually think that there's a simple way of avoiding the problem, even if it is "to cut off your nose to spite your face."

The Crowns, a middle-aged couple, regularly invested small sums in bonds and came into a windfall thanks to a sudden turn of the market. This would have been the right time to reconsider their investments, consult an expert, and change their lifestyle accordingly, indulging in a couple of things they had dreamed of since their youth.

Mr. Crown decided that they should visit a developer and move into a house with a garden and swimming pool and out of the small, dark apartment in which they had spent most of their married life. Mrs. Crown listened to him attentively, nodding at the better quality of life her husband envisaged for the years to come. When he finished laying out his plan, she said, "Sounds great, but I think it would be a mistake."

Asked to explain what she meant, she pinpointed that "both our families and friends, who cannot afford that kind of luxury, will barge in on us every weekend. The swimming pool will become a public facility, with kids splashing around to the point of exasperation. That garden you want to tend to won't get a chance; it will be trodden on beyond repair by our uninvited guests. And what about me? Should I become a full-time cook to feed them? No way."

Mr. Crown believed this was sheer madness, but when he spoke of his plan to his sister, her remarks set him thinking. "Oh, wouldn't that be wonderful!" she said. "What a relief to think that we'll have a cozy, private place to go on weekends, plus the added joy of gathering the family together on a regular basis! We don't see enough of each other, mostly because none of us has enough room to hold a proper reunion in a relaxed atmosphere, don't you think?"

It wasn't necessary for his wife to rub an "I told you so" into his face. The couple deprived themselves of what they had so long desired because they felt it would become "public" property.

What were the Crowns afraid of? Obviously, they feared intrusion, but also their own inability to set the limits. Thus, in their view, not having what others might also enjoy was preferable to being invaded or having a run-in with their relatives. Their narrow-mindedness painted the picture in black and white, with no shades in between. Their decision to leave things unchanged also discouraged them from seeking better, more profitable investments. What for, if they weren't going to enjoy the money anyway? You may think that this is a rare case. Believe me, it's much more common than you can possibly imagine. At times, it gets so bad that not even the first efforts at improving an economic situation are made, on the grounds that others will profit from your gains for free.

As you see, fear hides behind the weirdest masks. Apart from particular reasons and life histories, the different kinds of fear share one characteristic; namely, they stem from a lack of self-esteem and self-confidence. If you don't bring yourself to believe that you deserve the very best that life can offer and work toward it in the conviction that you will eventually meet your goals, no guru's financial advice will work for you. The secret, that secret that some claim to have unveiled and that others are seeking as if it were the now-in-fashion Grail, is your belief in your own capacity, intelligence, common sense, responsibility, and ability to make things happen. No "buts." The minute you let a "but" interfere with your determination, you have lost the power that engineers your success.

3.7
Success
Many of those who actually make money hand over fist owe it to other people's gullibility.

For reasons that escape me, some men and women love being lied to. Although they know that some things are impossible unless preceded by the right steps (and waiting for processes to mature happens to be one of such steps), they become mesmerized by false promises. No sooner does someone assure them that they can get "the big money" by just reaching out for it than they obediently follow whole sets of instructions in the sincere belief that they will succeed. This attitude somehow reminds one of the "learn French (or any other foreign language) in fifteen days" experience. Grown-up people with an education could be expected to remember how long it took them to learn the subjects in the curriculum, and how hard it proved to master some of them. Yet these very people jump at the "opportunity" to understand, speak, read, and write such a complex system as gives shape to whatever language. It never works. Still, the dejected learner grows disappointed in herself. "I didn't devote enough time to the lessons." "I wasn't perseverant." The target of these deceitful businesses is a subject well studied by the marketing departments that lead these sales campaigns. Their prey is he/she who believes in miracles, much as he/she denies it.

The general attitude to the "make money fast" techniques tends to mimic this behavior. The gurus of the day, all of them rich, sell their secrets wrapped between the covers of a book, lecture around the country, and persuade their audiences that their money came to them as a result of applying this or that methodology. The gullible individual invests in the book, devours its content, puts the advice received into practice and, when money doesn't come rolling in, blames herself for not having done things right. "I surely skipped something," she thinks. "I may have misunderstood." "It's not the system; it's just me." For if the guru did make heaps of money using this system, the failure cannot possible lie with the system.

Let me tell you an enlightening story to illustrate the "get rich quickly" kind of advice.

A Mr. So-and-so placed an advertisement in a widely read newspaper that read, "If you want to learn an infallible method to make a fortune, send a dollar to P.O. Box # . . . You will receive the material in two months."

The ad came out every day for one month. Millions of people all over the country sent their dollar. Wasn't it a real bargain to gain access to the secret for such a negligible amount? Punctually, when the second month had passed, Mr. So-and-so placed a really big, visible ad in the same newspaper. This time it read, "To get rich quickly, just do as I did."

What I'm trying to get across to you is that you need to clear your mind of magic thoughts. I assume that by now you have some clue to what has been preventing you from making money. Supposing none of the case histories and/ or explanations offered in this book fits your case, you'll resort to introspection to find out what's wrong with your inner self that stands in your way. Use the blank page/s at the end of this part to do so.

Once you've overcome your difficulties—something that will not happen until you can consciously identify them— you need to begin to work in the direction of money.

Do not let yourself be fooled. Do not take attractive shortcuts to your aim, for they are indeed attractive, but only to those who increase their purse at your expense.

Seek advice from serious, respectable advisors, and

brace yourself up to wait. Do not get caught into activities of which you know nothing. Do not entrust your (meager) savings to the Gekkos of this world. Above all, do not get greedy. Wise, safe investment and careful follow-up of the route the business you have chosen takes will eventually land you on the golden field of your dreams.

Remember that risk ventures (short term, high risk, can either pay great sums or leave you literally in the street) very much resemble the odds at a casino. An experienced gambler told me once that when you bet, never mind on what, you must be ready to lose and *not look back*. What he meant was that the money you gamble should be the money you can dispense with rather than the money that will keep you/your family going in acceptable terms.

Go out into the jungle and make money. But remember that this is hard work not a game.

As long as you take responsibility for your actions, do not endanger other people's prospects (your children's university tuition fees, for example), do not fall into the traps set by charlatans, and keep in mind exactly what you're doing and why, you're bound to succeed.

WHAT STANDS IN THE WAY BETWEEN ME AND MONEY?

Bibliography

Attali, Jacques: *Los judíos, el mundo, y el dinero: Historia económica del pueblo judío.* Fondo de Cultura Económica de España, S.L. España, 2005.

The Bible. http://www.bibleontheweb.com/Bible.asp

Dorgelis, Roland: *¡Pobres ricos!* En: Janus 9, Librería Hachette S.A., Buenos Aires, 1967.

Dostoevski, Fyodor: *Crime and Punishment.* Norton Critical Editions, New York, 1964.

Fiddler on the Roof. http://www.allmusicals.com/lyrics/americanmusical/iflwerearichman.htm

Freud, Sigmund: *Some Character Types Met With in Psycho-Analytic Work.* In: The Standard Edition of the Complete Psychological Works of Sigmund Freud, Vol. XIX. The Hogarth Press and the Institute of Psychoanalysis, London, 1975.

Gillet, Grant: *Philosophical Psychology.* Vol. 14, Issue 4, Dec. 2001 at http://www.informaworld.com/smpp/content=a713690544&db=all

Graves, Robert & Patai Raphael: *Hebrew Myths: The Book of Genesis.* Carcanet Press, Manchester, 2005.

Graves, Robert: *The Greek Myths.* Penguin Books, Great Britain, 1980.

Laplanche, J. and Pontalis J.B.:*Diccionario de Psicoanálisis.* Editorial Labor, Barcelona, 1981.

Milton, John: *Paradise Lost. Books I AND II.* Macmillan & Co. Ltd., New York—St. Martin's Press, 1962.

Plato: *The Republic.* Penguin Books, England, 2003.

Silberstein, Enrique: *El hombre ante la riqueza.* En: Janus 9, Librería Hachette S.A., Buenos Aires, 1967.

Sullerot, Evelyne: *Las mujeres y el dinero.* En: Janus 9, Librería Hachette S.A., Buenos Aires, 1967.

Weber, Max: *The Protestant Ethic and the Spirit of Capitalism.*BN Publishing, U.S.A., 2008.